# WHERE TO START BEFORE YOU START

*Seven Foundational Truths for Kingdom Entrepreneurs*

## Ben Hardman
## Dave Warner

**KDI Publishing**

Copyright © 2024 Kingdom Dreams Initiative

All rights reserved

The characters and events portrayed in this book are fictitious. Any similarity to real persons, living or dead, is coincidental and not intended by the author.

No part of this book may be reproduced, or stored in a retrieval system, or transmitted in any form or by any means, electronic, mechanical, photocopying, recording, or otherwise, without express written permission of the publisher.

ISBN-13: 9798329662368

Cover design by: Ali Hale Designs
Library of Congress Control Number: 2018675309
Printed in the United States of America

*This book is dedicated to all the dreamers seeking to change the world. It is our sincere hope that this pours fuel on the fire of your dreams in ways that you see flourishing and change in your communities. Your dream is important and we look forward to seeing it come to reality.*

# CONTENTS

Title Page
Copyright
Dedication
Prologue   1
Introduction   16
Why Foundational Truths?   24
Preparation   31
Foundational Truth #1   32
Foundational Truth #2   46
Process   59
Foundational Truth #3   60
Foundational Truth #4   71
Posture   83
Foundational Truth #5   84
Foundational Truth #6   94
Foundational Truth #7   105
Epilogue   116

# PROLOGUE

It was an ordinary day for Ram, age twenty-six. She and her mom busied themselves with the routine daily tasks of life in their rural village on the outskirts of Kathmandu in Nepal. The day was April 25, 2015, and their lives would be forever changed.

Shortly before noon, an earthquake escalating to 7.8 on the Richter Scale quickly ended the lives of 8,964 people and injured 21,952 more. Ram and her mother found themselves trapped in the chaos and debris of their collapsed house.

Not long after their eventual rescue by her brother, Mercy Corps came in to provide assistance and capture Ram's story. She said, "The top two stories of our house collapsed after the very first tremor. My mother and I were instantly trapped. It was so fast I can't even describe it. I don't have many scratches on my body but it hurts. I have a lot of back pain. I'm happy to be alive but so devastated our house is gone. At this moment I'm totally blind to the future. I'm just thinking about whether we can ever rebuild our house."

What Ram, her family, and millions of others went through that day was what Walter Brueggemann, the brilliant

Old Testament scholar and pastor, calls disorientation. It's where everything changes. Where the natural order of things has been disrupted. We no longer have control over the situation and no understanding of our new normal.

Ram was in a place of devastating disorientation. Everything around her was lost. Friends and family were gone. Her safe place of home was destroyed. She was completely disoriented.

Brueggeman says that the whole human experience is lived in three spaces: orientation, disorientation, and reorientation. (Walter Brueggeman - Praying the Psalms)

BRUEGGEMANN TRIANGLE

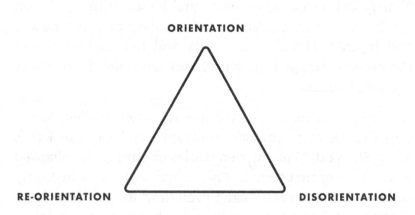

The first is a space of orientation. It is what we know: it is where all the rules are written and adhered to by everyone, and it's a place where we feel safe and secure, knowing that we can confidently navigate the world we are oriented to. That was everyday life in the village for Ram and her family. She would go about her daily tasks, to the market, to her job, to meet friends – normal activities of life. She knew how to navigate this world easily and securely. Her body, heart, soul, and mind were oriented to her everyday life.

But in a moment of disorientation, all the rules change, and all the things that used to work now suddenly no longer work. Ram's world was turned upside down, and nothing would ever be the same again. Even the place where she was most secure, her home, was destroyed, almost crushing her in the process.

BRUEGGEMANN TRIANGLE

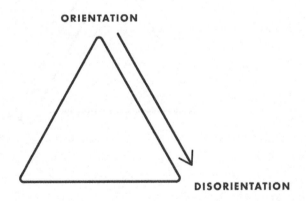

Her assessment immediately following the disaster captures something we all grapple with in the state of disorientation. She said, "At this moment, I'm totally blind to the future. I'm just thinking about whether we can ever rebuild our house."

She couldn't see forward, and she could not grapple with the future. She could only think about returning to her home if that was even possible. And that is the challenge of any season of disorientation. We have a simple choice: run from the unknown future and go back to the familiar, the known, go back to the place of orientation, or run into the unknown and trust that a promised land is available on the other side of disorientation.

BRUEGGEMANN TRIANGLE

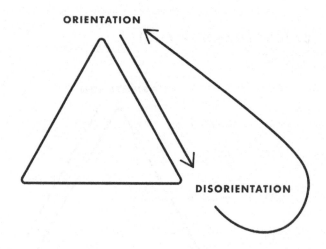

It is no secret that our society is in transition. Society is always in a state of change, but what we have seen since 2020 has hastened the pace and nature of change. During the early days of the COVID-19 pandemic, during lockdowns and shutdowns, people often said they just wanted to return to normal. They wanted to leave the disorientation of the pandemic and return to orientation, back to the old normal of what life used to be like.

Our natural inclination is to return to the relative safety of the old normal rather than navigate our way to a new normal. Our other natural tendency is to resist discomfort and pain. Unfortunately, change and transformation are almost always painful.

There is an awakening that occurs when one moves from orientation to disorientation. This awakening is because we recognize that even though we may not like it, a new normal now exists. While we prefer to be asleep in the old orientation – and we might even choose to go back to sleep – we must face the reality of our awakened situation to grapple with where God is guiding our path.

In the Book of Exodus, we see the Hebrew people under crushing oppression in their state of slavery. That was their orientation. For over four hundred years, they had been in bondage to Pharaoh and the Egyptian people. It was all they knew, all they understood, and all their bodies knew how to do. Then God interrupted time for them. God intervened, they escaped slavery, and went out into the wilderness. The wilderness was a Disorienting place for the Hebrew people. They didn't know how to live in the wilderness. Even though they were free, they were under a different kind of oppression.

They struggled for food and water, they struggled to learn the new rules and how to follow them. They struggled to trust the God they now followed in the wilderness. The Hebrews were utterly Disoriented.

When the Hebrews first awakened to their new situation, their first inclination was to go back to the place of orientation, Egypt, where they knew how things operated, and could at least have food and water. The Hebrews wanted to go back even though it was oppressive. Returning to the old normal seemed safer for many of them than wandering in the wilderness. They just wanted to go back to sleep.

There is a bit of revisionist history that takes place in disorientation. They were reminiscent of beds to sleep in and pots of meat to eat, but whatever fond memories they had of Egypt, the fact remained that they were enslaved. They would only experience complete identity change once they walked through the wilderness.

So wander they did. For forty years. They wandered around throughout the wilderness because they did not trust God to guide them into the Promised Land. At the same time, God reshaped them into a new identity that would give them the courage to take the Promised Land. They took a journey that should have lasted only eleven days to cross the wilderness and extended it to forty years.

Our choices in the wilderness determine our breakthrough in the promised land.

Unfortunately, we can't get to the promised land without going through the desert. How long we stay there, what paths we take, and whether we learn the lessons God has for us is entirely up to us, but make no mistake, God shapes us in the wilderness so we can become people of breakthrough in the promised land.

Richard Rohr aptly calls this phase the "liminal space," a threshold of transition and waiting, where we are suspended between the familiar and the completely unknown (Richard Rohr, introduction to Oneing 8, no.

1, Liminal Space (Spring 2020): 19). It is a time of not knowing as we bid farewell to the old world while unsure of what the new existence holds for us. One of my friends calls this space "the messy middle"—a fitting description for where we often find ourselves.

BRUEGGEMANN TRIANGLE

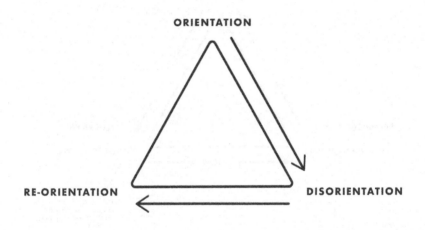

The process of working through disorientation is aligning us with the work and power of God. We are aligning with the identity God is creating within us. We align ourselves with God to do the work God has designed for us. Scripture calls this walking by faith or walking with the Spirit. This is the space in our lives where we previously had no direction, but now we are walking step by step with the Father. Alignment with God gives us access to His presence, power and our own potential grows. Whether this alignment is heart alignment and personal transformation or if it has to do with your business or or your future. Aligning our way with the Father is what leads us out of disorientation. We are aligning with the new realities of life around us. When we allow ourselves to go through the complex process of Orientation, Disorientation, and Reorientation, we also see that we become awake, aligned, and alive.

BRUEGGEMANN TRIANGLE

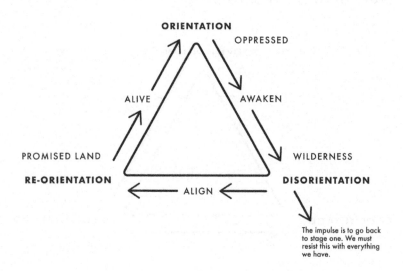

Gone are the unsettling days of disorientation. We've moved beyond the unfamiliar territory and found ourselves in a place that feels like a warm embrace. It's a moment of acceptance – a wholehearted embrace of the new normal. And in this acceptance, we recognize that God's guiding hand has led us here.

You are meant to live in the promised land, but so few of us ever arrive there. Instead, we settle for a life of mediocrity and live out lesser dreams and lesser identities than the one God has given us and named for us.

Perhaps you are in this state of disorientation right now. Like Ram, maybe your world has turned upside down, and the safest place you know of has started to feel more like a grave than a home. It may be difficult for you right now to see the future, and you long for a return to the old normal. You want to return to where it was safe and known, even if it was oppressive, like it was for the Hebrews.

You may have already come through the most challenging portion of disorientation and now see a clearer picture of what being alive looks like. The beauty of transformation is that we are never done. God is always inviting us back into orientation, back into re-alignment with Him. So the Bruggeman triangle is a path we walk over and over again until the day we die.

We believe that the seven Foundational Truths in this book are indispensable for any believer awakened and alive to the reorientation God is bringing into their life. We see these truths working in the life of an individual believer. We dream of thousands of individual believers living out the Foundational Truths as they seek to capture the promised land of God and become fully alive to the blessing God has for them.

The story of how our founder, Ben Hardman, started Kingdom Dreams Initiatives is a telling example of the Dreamer's journey from disorientation and awakening to reorientation and coming alive! The story goes something like this...

I (Ben) had finally decided to go out on my own. After nearly twenty years as a leadership consultant and a coach working for various organizations, developing young leaders, creating healthy cultures, and building for sustainability, the day had come when I needed a change. I had been through a season of immense occupational disorientation. It was not that I did not love the work I was doing or even that I did not love the clients I was working with. I kept feeling as if there was more for me. The things that used to make me come alive felt a bit boring. The doors that used to swing open were all closing. The grace was running out for me, and things that did not bother me in the past were driving me crazy.

I had an immense feeling of restlessness that maybe something out there for me would lead to more fulfillment and even more breakthroughs for the leaders I serve. So I did it. I left the consulting organization I had spent many years building and developing. I stopped all my consulting and coaching and started saying no when anyone asked me to coach for their organization. I was starting something new and going out on my own. I was going to launch Kingdom Dreams Initiative (KDI), a start-up incubator for everyday people. I would spend the second half of my life helping Christian leaders launch their kingdom dreams. I was both excited and terrified!

I did what most entrepreneurs would do. I spent months preparing. In fact, many of the tools we use in our start-up incubators now were the tools I began using and creating as I was building KDI. I talked to customers. I worked through defining the problems we solved. I built a team. I created an MVP (minimum viable product). I built out my business model canvas. I created a brand and brand identity. I made a website and a landing page. I created a compelling product and offer. I started sharing my journey on social media. I created a mailing list of around eight hundred friends and former clients who were interested in the work I was creating. I started BETA testing our coaching process locally and quietly for over a year, and we started seeing actual results and real breakthroughs for these local clients in not only their business but in their lives.

I started working with dreamers with a kingdom dream they wanted to launch. We believe that a kingdom dream is the good work that God has implanted within you. Ephesians 2:10 talks about the good work God has created in advance for you. It's kind of like your occupation, the thing that sustains you as you work in it.

As I built out KDI, a venture fund approached me and asked me to pitch at their demo day. They highlighted the top twenty-five ideas that could change the church in the next twenty-five years, and they loved the concept of KDI. I was awarded a small amount of seed funding on that pitch day to get started. The fact that people saw value in what we are doing is the reason I am passionate about helping leaders in our start-up incubators create a compelling pitch and presentation at our pitch days. That small amount of money I received propelled KDI into the future and allowed me to start. That pitch day is why we have a nonprofit foundation that comes alongside under-resourced kingdom leaders to help them get the training and resources they need to launch their kingdom dream.

In preparing to launch, I sent emails for months. I invited everyone I knew to a launch day event we were doing online. All of this was in the middle of COVID-19, which may not have been the best time to launch a business, but I pressed on. I planned an amazing webinar. I started inviting people into our first incubator, which was open to the public. I was obnoxious about asking friends and family to help spread the word and support the work. I thought I had built years of reciprocity as a pastor and a consultant, and that everyone I knew would be willing and excited to help me launch! I had planned word for word what I would say and how we would invite our audience into my offer, and I would instantly start converting sales.

I did not sleep the night before the launch because there was something terribly vulnerable about launching out on my own. In every other job I had, there was an organization or another leader to hide behind. I was always the number-two, and other leaders filled the first seat. I had so much terrible internal stress, thinking, "if this fails, then do I fail?" I started asking myself all the "what-if" questions, and the stress and worry became too much for me. I stayed up late that night prepping, praying, hoping, and dreaming about what the next day would look like. I set my expectation that we would have three to five hundred people attend conservatively. And I expected we would sign up five to ten for our first incubator and we would double the size of my eight hundred-person mailing list in one event.

After much anticipation, the moment came, and I went live. I started sharing and watched the viewer count grow 1… 2… 5… 10… 15… 20… 25. Then it stopped growing. No one else joined. Five minutes later, the viewer count started declining as people started leaving 25… 20… 15… 10… 5.

Five people were left at the end of our webinar, and no one signed up for anything. I did not make a single sale. I didn't increase our mailing list by a single person, and I was right in the middle of disorientation. All that work, months of preparation, and my giant release celebration had instead become a massive pity party for me.

I am sure those who do internet marketing and are experts in webinars and product launches could critique my process (I was really bad at it). But at that moment, all I thought was, "What have I just done?"

I had just left a successful and growing consulting company I co-owned for this. My dream, the thing I believed God had called me to, and everything I had planned, thought through, and worked on for months had utterly failed.

I had two choices:
1. Run back to what I know and understand and beg for my job back at my consulting company (rush back to orientation from my wilderness of Disorientation).
2. Press on, pivot, learn, grow, and enter the desert of launching something new (move forward to align with what God was doing to come alive in Reorientation).

Since you are reading this now, you know I pressed on and kept working and building and developing. I kept learning and stretching, and slowly, we started to make progress. In my experience, this is how growth and development happens. It is not an overnight success or a one-time event; it's a series of small movements in the same direction that produce small results over time. It is one relationship at a time, one lesson learned each day, and continual commitment to get better each day. I'm so glad I didn't quit the first time I hit a wall of disorientation. In fact, as I look back over the last two years, this was the first of many setbacks, and I am so glad I didn't allow my kingdom dream to die the first time.

I believe we are stewards of not just our money, time and talents. We are stewards of God's dreams! I believe God has deposited a kingdom dream into every believer. It is that good work prepared for us in advance that we are called to in Ephesians 2.

It is a true joy when we get to live into and see God's dreams come to life. Grace Marietta where I pastored for years was God's dream for our community. KDI was God's dream for other dreamers and entrepreneurs. I've often wondered how many dreams die because of a lack of resources and training. I imagine there is a graveyard of dreams that God tried to deposit in us but we simply couldn't stir up the imagination to make it happen. We want to provide the right kind of training so the imagination of dreamers is stirred to make dreams a reality.

In our first two years at KDI, we launched one hundred and five successful kingdom ventures. We worked with over five hundred kingdom entrepreneurs, and we were able to give away over $75,000 of support and services to early-stage dreamers who need resources and training. I'm so glad I didn't run back to Egypt. I'm so thankful I didn't beg for my old job back. I'm also so glad that along the way, I learned the foundational truths you will find in this book.

These foundational truths have been critical growth components for our team at KDI and many of our start-up incubator participants. They have helped train, develop, and launch amazing non-profit organizations that bring social and community changes to communities. They have been the catalyst for launching many for-profit organizations that bring economic change to communities and produce jobs and dignity for the leaders involved.

They have created many ministries and micro-churches, bringing spiritual transformation to countless leaders. They have also been a wayfinding tool for me. They are the principles I turn to when I feel I need more support. When I don't know what to do, I look to these foundational truths. They are the truths I wish I had my whole career and are where to start before you start anything.

# INTRODUCTION

*The Four Challenges Every Entrepreneur Faces and Why Foundational Truths Are Helpful*

Working with hundreds of leaders, we have found that every entrepreneur consistently faces the same challenges when beginning their start-up. While many more issues are unique to each start-up, we see these four as the most consistent challenges everyone faces. Every time we face a new challenge, we can either back down or rise to the challenge and adopt a new skill.

## The 4 Challenges

**1) Lack of entrepreneurial training and development.**

Much has been written about the challenges of entrepreneurship. The reality is that 80% of new businesses fail. Eight out of ten don't make it past the first year. Ideas are a dime a dozen. We believe that the best idea wins, but you need far more than just a good idea to launch your dream. In Michael Gerber's book *The E Myth* and later,

*The E Myth Revisited*, he talks about how many of us get into entrepreneurship because we have a particular technical skill that we are good at.

You bake the best cookies, so you open a bakery.
You are a great artist, so you open a gallery.
You are terrific at serving people experiencing poverty, so you open a non-profit.
You are a great coach and consultant, so you open your own agency.

The challenge is that you must continue to bake the best cookies, create the best art, and be a great coach and consultant. You also have to learn a whole new set of skills around running a business or non-profit. These skills are far more complicated to learn than you imagine and are often realized only when you go through the fire of launching your first venture. This is the challenge every early-stage dreamer runs into. I got into this because I am great at "Y," and now all I find myself doing is "Z."

So what you need is a new set of skills: you need training and development.

In Tod Bolsinger's brilliant book, *Canoeing the Mountains*, he uses the metaphor of Lewis and Clark to describe the disorientation many leaders feel in post-Christian culture. (citation) Lewis and Clark were prepared to canoe through the rivers and waterways to discover a passage to the Pacific Ocean. They were experts in these rivers and waterways and had a plan and an idea of how they could canoe to the Pacific Ocean. The problem was they ran into the Rocky Mountains. Canoes can't make it over mountains, and all of Lewis and Clark's expertise in navigating waterways was useless.

They had to adapt.
They had to learn new skills.
They needed new guides to train them to adapt to their new world.

The same principle is true for entrepreneurs and dreamers. What got you to this place may not get you through this space! So, where will you turn to help you navigate the mountains and the disorientation you face? Dreams are dying because leaders like you need guides, they need to learn new skills, and they don't know where to turn to help navigate the mountains and deserts in their paths.

## 2) Lack of Funding and Resources

My (Ben) son is a Junior in College this year, and he just rented his first home with some of his friends at college. I'm so proud of the young man he is becoming, and it has been interesting to watch him learn the value of money over the last few years. He sat down with me over the summer and said, "Dad, I'm sorry that I took for granted all of the gifts you gave us as kids and how hard you worked to provide us with all we needed." He shared that he didn't realize how much I had sacrificed for him until he got out on his own and had to pay his own bills. He said, "This was all a lot easier when you paid for everything."

This is also the challenge of starting something new. I used to be great at being a Monday morning quarterback. I was great at being the one who criticized the boss about how money was spent, how strategy was lived out, how culture was developed, and how tough decisions were made. Hindsight was always a gift for me that the leaders I served didn't have. I could watch mistakes made, and then, after the fact, I could critique all the choices.

The term for this is Fundamental Attribution error or attribution effect. The principle simply teaches us that we often underemphasize situational and environmental factors for the behavior of an actor while overemphasizing dispositional or personality factors. In other words we give ourselves the benefit of the doubt that we don't give to others. All that changed when I needed to come up with dollars to pay staff, cover the bills, and launch new initiatives. All that changed when I didn't have the benefit of second-guessing because I had to make the tough decisions.

I see dreams die every day because of inadequate financial plans, assumptions, and a general lack of access to finances. To launch your dream will take finances. We often live in an imaginary world where we believe financing is easier to find than we think and that if we create real *"Impact,"* then real *"Income"* will always follow. A lot of misguided coaches and consultants teach this idea.

Many kingdom leaders we work with are great at creating impact. They know how to get results and produce meaningful kingdom work that makes the world a better place. They are amazing at what they do. The problem is they need a real plan for making their work sustainable. They don't have access to funding and don't have a plan to get there. So, one to two years into their venture, they are making a difference for a small number of people, but they have to close the doors because they never developed a strategic plan for sustainability.

The majority of dreamers we work with are here. They have a great idea and the skills to make it happen; they even have a plan to make a difference. They don't have the access and skills to create income.

Entrepreneurs know the difference between a strategic plan on paper and a lived out business plan. Typically, it's blood sweat and tears in the process. Numbers on a paper do not mean finances in the bank account. We need leaders who are willing to develop a plan but also willing to do the hard work needed to create sustainable income.

We want to help dreamers create income *and* impact. We want you to make a difference and make a living. We have watched far too many ministries and non-profits produce excellent results yet need help to pay the bills every month. We have watched far too many businesses launch with a wonderful plan only to underestimate the financial realities and close the door and become another number in the 80% of failed businesses.

Dreams are dying because leaders like you need a plan not only for creating an impact but also for creating income.

### 3) Lack of an Accountable Process

As I launched KDI, the one thing I learned from my years of consulting and coaching was that leaders need tools, and leaders need a proven process. You don't simply need a strategy, you need an operating system. My wife is a business analyst for a large bank. She works with the leaders on the business side of her company to develop software and strategies to make life easier for the leaders on the ground. She interacts with those leaders doing the work and with coders and developers who write the code to develop new tools to make life easier for the business. As she stepped deeper into her role, she realized that she needed to learn a new language of coding to understand the challenges of developing new software for her users.

She not only needed the business language, she needed the coding language. So, she has been taking college classes to learn this new language of coding.

For many kingdom leaders, there is a new language or a new operating system that needs to be learned and developed. Few leaders are humble enough to learn a new language or operating system. We want to stick with the one that got us here. The best way to learn a new language is when someone teaches you, someone who knows how to speak and someone who knows the way. You need someone to show you the way and teach you a new way, much like the people of God in the wilderness needed to learn a new identity. We need to learn an accountable process to create income and impact. There have been many moments as an entrepreneur where I have said, "I wish someone would just tell me what to do." Entrepreneurship is like a game with one million different moves, possibilities and options each day. Choosing the best option often feels impossible!

We get these questions nearly every day:
- What should I do next?
- Where should I be putting my energy today?
- What is the most important thing I should be working on today?
- What is my next step?
- I'm so overwhelmed! Help!

Sometimes, you need to borrow someone else's playbook. Sometimes, you need a project manager to help you with the next steps. Sometimes, you need someone who has been there before to give you directions.

Dreams are dying because leaders don't have an accountable process to follow.

**4) Lack of Community and Relationships**
I had a call a few weeks back with an incredibly successful entrepreneur friend. On the outside, his life and ministry look amazing. He has a beautiful family, and his social media feed looks way more fun than mine. He is taking great trips, laughing with great people, and eating at great places. His business also looks impressive. They are growing fast, creating more income than ever, and making a real difference for their clients. But at the end of our conversation, he said, "I'm so lonely. I may not be cut out for entrepreneurship because I feel so alone every day." This is not uncommon for entrepreneurs. According to CEO Today magazine, over 73% of entrepreneurs admit to feeling lonely regularly, and over 60% of leaders say they have no community to turn to when things get tough. Steve Noble, Chief Operating Officer at Ultimate Finance, commented: "It's hugely concerning to hear how widespread loneliness is in the business community. I talk to business owners daily, and this research backs up what I already know – that they feel stressed and isolated. Although these feelings can be an unavoidable reality of running a company, it's clear that more help should be available." I remember challenging days when I was asking questions like:

- Who do I call to get help on this issue?
- I don't know how to find the answer to this challenge and don't know who to ask.
- I wish there was someone I could process this with.
- I should find a partner even if they aren't a good fit because I'm so lonely.

Dreams are dying because entrepreneurs and dreamers don't have a community to belong to and relationships to guide them.

With all these challenges (and many more that we did not highlight), it can seem like the future is bleak for anyone starting up a new thing. But there is hope! The 7 Foundational Truths can be a guide to help you through the challenges of entrepreneurship.

# WHY FOUNDATIONAL TRUTHS?

In the following chapters, you will find seven Foundational Truths to help guide you and your community into an awakening to come Alive to the Reorientation of your Kingdom Dream.

A foundation is a set of principles that a person lives by. It's the reason *why* you do what you do. It's the guide for the practice and actions of your life. A foundation is a set of values that provide the reason for being and living.

In the construction industry, foundations have a similar role. While it is rarely, if ever seen, the foundation is the most essential part of any building or structure. Foundations in buildings have these primary roles:

1. Bear the load
2. Anchor the structure
3. Isolate outside influences
4. Plumb the walls

Foundations are vital to every building because they bear the weight of all the structures and activities that will be built above them. There is vital work to be done on and in the building that can't be done if the foundation is weak and unable to bear the load of the work.

Without a secure foundation, a building is susceptible to natural forces that work against it, such as earthquakes, tornadoes, and hurricanes. A secure foundation will anchor the building to withstand those elements that seek to destroy the structure while it is being built and long after completion.

Ground moisture is one of the greatest enemies of a building and its foundation. A good foundation will isolate the forces of moisture to keep the building free from the outside influences of swelling, shrinking, freezing, and thawing.

These key characteristics of a good foundation: bearing, anchoring, and isolating are the same characteristics that should be found in the foundation of your life and your start-up for business and ministry – to keep you on the right track of your Kingdom Dream.

**1. Bear the Load** – You carry an enormous (and frequently lonely) weight as a leader and an entrepreneur. You cannot carry this weight without a strong foundation underneath you. Part of your foundation can (and should) include other people so that you have companionship in your work and gain from the collective wisdom of others. Without a strong foundation, you might begin to see cracks under the stressful weight of your responsibilities and work.

**2. Anchor the Structure** – As a leader, you may have a

target on your back from people who don't want to see you succeed. They want nothing more than for you to fail and remove your competition from their market. A secure foundation will anchor you so that when the challenges buffet you, you will find a secure anchor that keeps you from being pushed beyond the point of breaking.

It's not just nefarious forces working against you; the market can work against you, too. Navigating market forces during uncertain and unusual times without a secure anchor will cause you to chase every new idea and potentially keep you from accomplishing your mission and realizing your dream. The Foundational Truths will keep you anchored!

3. **Isolate Outside Influences** – You have a vision, a dream God has given you. This is your precious gift; you do not want to be tainted by outside influences. A good foundation will protect your dream from losing its vitality to external pressure and influences.

Good foundations are vital to any structure to help you bear the weight of your responsibilities, anchor you in times of stress, and isolate outside influences so you are not distracted from your vision and can pursue your dream to its full realization.

4. **Plumb the Walls** – You want to do things right and do the right things. A good foundation will keep your life and start-up "plumb." Plumb is the building term for level. A good foundation keeps you straight and true. It keeps your walls square. It keeps you from leaning into yourself too far and from leaning too far outside yourself. A good foundation will keep you upright and allow you to have integrity throughout your long life of entrepreneurialism.

Everyone has a foundation. Some can articulate their foundation, some cannot; some foundations are strong, secure, sealed, and plumbed, while other foundations are weak, insecure, and susceptible to outside forces.

There is grave danger in a weak foundation, whether in construction or life, because any mistakes made in your foundation will get worse as you build up. This is called the ***principle of compounding defects***. If the foundation is imperfect and the first course is not laid perfectly, the rest of the structure will increasingly fail as you move upward.

If you build on a weak or insecure foundation, your walls will never be plumb and true, and you will have a more challenging time fitting your door. Your windows won't operate properly, and your roof will inevitably leak. Everything you build on a shaky foundation is subject to trouble when you build on an insecure foundation.

At the end of the Sermon on the Mount in Matthew chapter 7, Jesus briefly speaks to this principle of building on a solid and secure foundation:

*24 "Everyone then who hears these words of mine and does them will be like a wise man who built his house on the rock. 25 And the rain fell, and the floods came, and the winds blew and beat on that house, but it did not fall because it had been founded on the rock.* (ESV)

Look how the outside forces impacted this house built on a secure foundation. The rain fell, floods came, winds blew and beat on the house, and it was unshaken – because of its strong, secure, sealed foundation.

But then Jesus contrasts this with someone who builds

their house on an insecure foundation:

*26 And everyone who hears these words of mine and does not do them will be like a foolish man who built his house on the sand. 27 And the rain fell, and the floods came, and the winds blew and beat against that house, and it fell, and great was the fall of it."* (ESV)

When some outside forces came against the house built on an insecure foundation, it fell apart – and great was its fall!

Houses built on an insecure foundation have weaknesses that will be paid for later. There will be a fall. There will be a price to pay.

We don't want you to fall. We don't want the principle of compounding defects to catch up with you. We want to help you with Seven Foundational Truths that have come out of our lives that have guided and helped us along the way and can help you on your journey to the Promised Land as well.

But like Jesus, you should not only hear (or read) these words but also apply them. Hearing is good, but doing it in conjunction with hearing is better! Jesus said the wise person will Hear and Do.

The Seven Foundational Truths are only as good as their application, so at the end of each chapter, you will find some practical questions that you can ponder and reflect on your own or with your team. There will even be some steps you can take towards awakening your kingdom dream. We recommend doing this in community in partnership with a few like-minded folks that will be a part of your foundation.

Our prayer is that these truths will help you awaken the dream that you have within you, whether it's a new dream, a dormant dream, or a dream that you've had but stalled out because you didn't have the right next steps to take. We pray that these truths will help you awaken your community to address the key problems to build a culture of redemptive entrepreneurship in your world.

We want to help you take steps, even if they are micro-steps, to make progress to make your dream a reality so you don't lose heart and fall short of launching.

The Seven Foundational Truths will help you build that strong, secure, sealed foundation so that as you take the next steps in your kingdom dream, you will be like the wise man who built his house on the rock.

We've organized the truths into three helpful categories with two truths each to illustrate every entrepreneur's journey:

**Preparation**
This is what you need to learn and adopt before you begin. Before you start chasing the dream, do this work.

**Process**
These truths will help you while you are on your journey to keep a steady pace and not burn out.

**Posture**
These truths will give you staying power in your work and help you build lasting relationships.

Our seventh and final truth encapsulates the spirit of all the truths together, but we ask you to resist the urge to skip the end. Instead, take your time with each truth. Consider making this a devotional journey and reading just one chapter a day. Or one chapter a week and try to adopt the truth into your everyday life.

# PREPARATION

*This is what you need to learn and adopt before you begin! Before you start chasing the dream, do this work!*

# FOUNDATIONAL TRUTH #1

*Service over Strategy: Fall in Love with The Problem, Not Your Solution*

> "Fall in love with the problem, not the solution."
>
> KAAREN HANSON

> So the Jews said, "See how he loved him!"
>
> JOHN 11:36

Whitcomb Judson (1843-1909) was an engineer, salesman, inventor and a good friend who could see a need and solve a problem. One of Judson's best friends' body ached after a lifetime of literal back-breaking labor. With each movement Judson's friend found himself becoming more and more limited. A sudden jolt of pain would send him reeling, discovering that he could no longer move this way or make that motion. Safe medication did not exist at that time for him to find relief so this man had to rely on family and friends, like Whitcomb Judson, for assistance for even the most menial of tasks.

The year was 1891, and it was the peak of the Gilded Age, where innovation was taking the nation by storm and yet, some industries were limited to technology that was thousands of years old. Such was the case for the fashion industry that relied on an old-fashioned design to fasten every piece of clothing from shoes to overcoats: the button. And so, every time this back-pain-laden man bent over to undertake the laborious task of buttoning his shoes, he was reminded of how feeble his body was.

At least until Whitcomb Judson entered the scene.

This dutiful friend saw the daily struggle of the simple, yet inconvenient and painful act of putting on and buttoning shoes. Judson fell in love with the problem, as it were, and worked to develop a solution whereby his pain-ridden friend could fasten his own shoes without the fumbling of buttons.

Whitcomb Judson fashioned a pair of shoes with a sliding fastener that he patented as the "clasp-locker". Ultimately, the clasp-locker would undergo many iterations and improvements as Judson fine-tuned his solution to perfect it for the problem at hand. It took decades for Judson's clasp-locker to become a fashion-fastening staple, but once it did, what became known as the "Zipper" became a ubiquitous device for form and function in nearly every possible article of clothing.

The zipper started as a solution for one man's painful problem: he could not bend over to button his shoes. Whitcomb Judson's empathetic curiosity to find the right solution for his friend became a game-changing device for the global fashion industry.

Not to mention the many varied uses of zippers today, where they are found in places from tents in the backwoods all the way to pressurized suits designed for outer space.

Suppose Judson's life goal was to change global fashion forever? What if his strategy was to create something that would be the next big thing in Paris? What if he had ignored the plight of his friend in order to reach for a loftier goal than to merely serve someone in need?

To understate the obvious, the likelihood of his ability to influence global fashion trends would be greatly diminished. Instead, he had a goal to serve his friend and in the process created a device that would ultimately impact the entire world. Judson emphasized service over strategy.

One of the biggest problems we see dreamers face is that their dreams die because they don't solve a real problem for real people. Their dream is useless. Dreamers have big ideas and big passions and they want to make a big impact, but it never goes far unless it solves a real problem for real people.

In the excitement of trying to change the world for lots of people, one of our incubator participants built out a three-year curriculum for spiritual coaching. However, they didn't have any participants. Their enthusiasm drew them to a strategy, but no one was being served by it. Our counsel to this enthusiastic leader was to just build out three weeks of content and see if he could get one or two participants to try for free. The idea is to serve people first; to serve real people with real problems.

Whitcomb Judson's passion for the problem to serve his friend ended up changing the world for the better. This is what kingdom dreamers do! One life at a time, we change the world for the better.

Even if it is just one life that is changed.

In John chapter 11 we find the story of Lazarus. Jesus is hanging out with the disciples when Lazarus' sisters send word to Jesus that Lazarus was sick. Instead of leaving to go see Lazarus right that moment, or even better yet, healing Lazarus on the spot from where he was, Jesus lingered two more days in that place. After those two long days had passed, Jesus decided to take the disciples to visit Lazarus.

When Jesus and the 12 finally arrive, they discover that Lazarus had already been dead and buried in a tomb for four days. They are greeted by the mourning villagers and one of the deceased's sisters, Mary, who comes to Jesus weeping and saying, "Lord, if you had been here, my brother would not have died."

We pick it up at John 11:33-36 (ESV)

*33 When Jesus saw her weeping, and the Jews who had come with her also weeping, he was deeply moved in his spirit and greatly troubled. 34 And he said, "Where have you laid him?" They said to him, "Lord, come and see." 35 Jesus wept. 36 So the Jews said, "See how he loved him!"*

Jesus felt the pain of Lazarus' sisters, Mary and Martha. Indeed, he felt the pain of all those who were in mourning as he empathetically mourned with them because Jesus loved Lazarus too. Jesus loved the one who had suffered the most.

So what did Jesus do? What was Jesus' unique solution to this universal problem? He called Lazarus to come out! Jesus reversed the problem of death and brought Lazarus back to life! Now we certainly don't expect you to raise anyone from the dead, but the foundational truth remains that we increase empathy through curiosity in effort to fall in love with the problem, not your solution. We believe it is the intersection of empathy and curiosity where we find our solutions.

EMPATHY + COMPASSION = SOLUTIONS

Exercising empathetic curiosity requires us to be in relationship with others. We have to talk to people. We must go out and see for ourselves what problems others are facing. Jesus stayed for two days in his location before going to see Mary, Martha, and Lazarus. And once he did, *then* he was moved with compassion to solve their problem.

As a Kingdom Dreaming entrepreneur, you are likely an expert in daydreaming. As we catch a glimpse of a solution, we begin running beautiful dreams through our minds all day. We become so excited about the Person God has created us to be, the Passion God has given us to pursue, and the Problem God has designed us to solve.

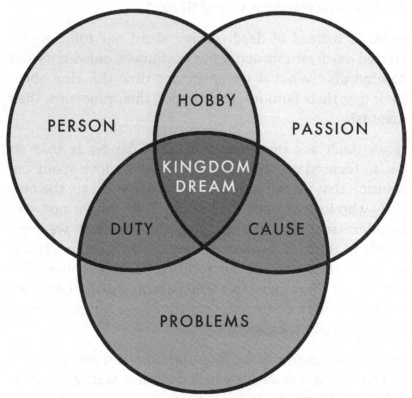

In our dreams, we see the innovative business we want

to start, the non-profit that could change the world, the church that will disciple the next generation. It is the thing that keeps us up at night and gets us up in the morning.

In your mind, you've already seen the future. Maybe you've imagined your dream one, five, or ten years down the road. You see the end goal. You see *the thing* that will be the solution to all of the problems in your life and the lives of those around you. The problem with this is that we can tend to have an insular focus on ourselves and not on the problems other people have.

The question we need to ask ourselves is, "what if we are daydreaming about the wrong thing?"

What if, instead of daydreaming about our solution, we started daydreaming about our customers, our clients, our community? What if we spent our time thinking about their day, their families, their hopes, their problems, their dreams?

If we don't ask these questions, the danger is that we get so focused on ourselves and what we love about our solution that we fail to realize that maybe we are the only ones who love or need that solution! We might not even be addressing someone else's needs! Too often we see a problem, think of a solution, and we transactionally and strategically try to sell our solution. Let's be honest. The world isn't short on people who post on social media their outrage around a problem that they have no intention of ever doing anything about.

And that is when we stop learning from and stop listening to people. Our advice for you is don't just start a business, solve a problem!

If you have a Kingdom Dream, it should solve real-world problems for real people, not just merely being a blessing for ourselves. We are the conduit for other people to be blessed. We are the sent ones through whom God will reduce someone's pain or bring them gain.

Kaaren Hanson, the former Director of Innovation at Intuit, is credited with coining the phrase, "Fall in love with the problem, not the solution." This phrase has become a mantra for the development and design world in many areas of industry. We have innovated on this phrase because we recognize that God does have a singular solution for all of our problems, so our suggestion is to not fall in love with *your* solution.

We must be open to the movement of God through the Holy Spirit. In other words, there may be more than just *your* solution to the problem you have discovered.

For Jesus and the story of Lazarus being raised from the dead, it is possible that there were many other solutions at Jesus' disposal to bring comfort to Mary, Martha, the village and even Himself.

Raising Lazarus from the dead just happened to be the solution that Jesus chose.

It may be important to note here that even this solution was not permanent. Eventually Lazarus died again. Eventually people mourned his loss all over again. There's no record of it in Scripture, but we know that he and his sisters did not live forever. Some solutions only provide temporary relief, but they do change the world for that person for a period of time.

And *that* is what we are trying to do: Change the world for people.

We have had many people who have gone through Kingdom Dreams Initiative report back that the users of their start-ups are saying things like, "Wow, you actually solved a problem that I had...you actually thought of me." Or one of my favorite comments, "you are giving words to all the things I have been thinking about." Ultimately, this is what we want for you and hopefully what *you* want for you. You want to bring healing, wholeness, and connection through the service you provide or the product you develop.

* * *

At Kingdom Dreams Initiative, we help people clearly define the problem they are seeing in our four-month Start-up Incubator. One of our amazing Incubator graduates, Chris served in various levels in the US Military. Moving from base to base every couple of years, Chris knows first hand how difficult it is to settle into a new community so quickly and so often. So Chris saw this problem for real people and decided to create a solution to help military members move from base to base and settle into new communities quickly.

Through our KDI Start-up Incubator, Chris worked on an app that he calls Brigade Ministries. Brigade Ministries helps military members make the transition from one base to the next to be in relationships with fellow believers in new locations quickly and efficiently. It links people to resources in the community including churches, local Bible

Studies with the hope of connecting people to one another and to their community.

When you fall in love with the problem, you keep listening and you keep being curious. Your empathy continues to grow. Chris works hard to clearly identify what is most helpful to the military members who are on the move. Compassionately curious questions help you to dig deeper to find out not only what the problem is, but also *why* someone is having that problem.

Compassionately curious questions lead people to open-ended answers that help you understand, to the best of your ability, the full scope of the problem they are encountering. You don't want to solve a problem your community or customer doesn't have!

What if Jesus had decided to multiply loaves and fishes while he was with the mourners at Lazarus' tomb? What if Jesus had decided to turn water into wine? That would have made for a great funeral meal, but that would not have been the solution to their problem at the time!

We all know about people who have fallen in love with their solution and we get tired of them talking about it because we might not even care about the problem they've identified *or* the solution they've developed!

But when you encounter someone who has fallen in love with a problem, you see them caring deeply, about people and about struggles people are having. Just like the people in the village noticed how much Jesus cared for Lazarus, you know that compassionately curious people care about you, and aren't just trying to make a sale. People with empathetic curiosity think more critically and more deeply about solving that problem. This is the posture of redemptive entrepreneurship; it is a deep care and empathy towards the people you serve.

It is important to note that the problems we speak of aren't necessarily as simple (or complex) as pain points. Yes, we can solve pain points for people but we also can provide gains for people. We can add to people's lives in areas that they might not even be aware they have a lack! The question then becomes: How can we mitigate someone's pain and add to someone's gain?

Maybe someone else is already attempting to solve this problem but you have discovered a way to solve it faster, cheaper, or more effectively. The bigger the problem you solve, the larger your audience will be. We believe entrepreneurial thinking combined with the Spirit of God living and working in you should solve the greatest problems that exist in the world. The people of God should be the first ones to solve social problems in our world.

Throughout the Gospels we find Jesus as the ultimate problem solver. Jesus never once solved a problem that wasn't actually a problem for the person he was connecting with. Healing the lepers, making the lame walk, giving sight to the blind, feeding the hungry, Jesus always tailored his solution to the problem of the individual and the corporate body. And yet, even in the midst of that unique problem-solving construct, Jesus made room to solve the problem experienced by all humanity: the need for redemption back into the family of God.

In the end, solving a physical problem was the open doorway through which Jesus solved a spiritual problem for each encounter he had with people. Jesus redeemed people spiritually while solving a physical problem.

Your Kingdom Dream, at its core, is to redeem people into relationship with Jesus, to bring them back to a sense of completeness and wholeness with God. Thankfully, God has created you to be a unique Person to pursue a particular Passion that will solve specific Problems that other people have. Through this unique blend, you will get to be a part of someone's redemption story.

## Apply Foundational Truth #1: Empathy Canvas

To apply the foundational truth 'Fall in Love with the Problem not your solution = Service over Strategy', have empathy for your customers, clients, or congregants.

The practical tool to integrate this foundational truth into your life is the Empathy Canvas pictured above. It is a tool you can use to better understand your customers to better serve them.

Use an Empathy Canvas to make an explicit profile of your customers to clarify your understanding of their needs and situation. The Empathy Canvas consists of five different areas you can use to map your customer understanding.

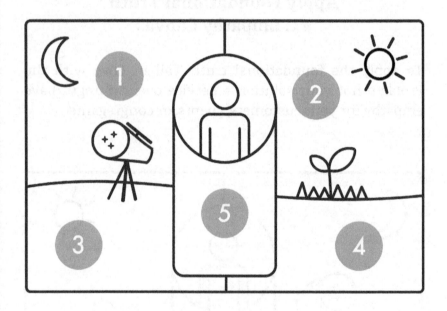

## 1 - Challenges

What keeps your customers up at night?
What are they worried about?
What problems are they hoping to solve?

## 2 - Motivations

What gets them up in the morning?
What makes them excited?
What gives them energy?

## 3 - Dreams

What are their goals for the future?
What do they hope to see changed in the world?
What redemptive longings do they

## 4 - Pains

What are their daily headaches?
What are their needs?
What negative things are they experiencing?

## 5 - Avatar

List the top 5 characteristics of your customer profile

# FOUNDATIONAL TRUTH #2

*Faith over Hustle: God Has Plenty of Resources*

> "God's work done in God's way will never lack God's supplies."
>
> HUDSON TAYLOR

> And the Lord will guide you continually and satisfy your desire in scorched places and make your bones strong; and you shall be like a watered garden, like a spring of water, whose waters do not fail.
>
> ISAIAH 58:11

When he packed his lunch that morning, he had no idea what he would see by the end of the day. He had heard there was a local phenomenon coming to his neck of the woods and a crowd gathering around. Even though he was just a young boy, he knew he didn't want to miss the excitement of this opportunity, so he took just enough provisions to sustain himself throughout the day's heat. For him, it was just a couple mile's walk outside of town to the large meadow on the hillside where people were already gathering.

He had heard stories about the mysterious man he was about to see. This man was one-part teacher, one-part storyteller, and one-part circus ringleader. Everyone wanted to see what unbelievable thing he would do next. Everyone wanted to hear what he would say next. Everyone wanted to learn from this teacher, including our young boy.

As the day wore on, the crowd started to grow. People of all ages were coming to hear the man speak. Estimates of up to 15,000 people were on that hillside to see the show, but they didn't know what would happen next.

Late in the day, the speaker took a short break and huddled with his team. The team members reminded the speaker that it had been a long day without a break, and everyone was hungry with no place to get food. The team all agreed that the speaker should provide a meal for the crowd, but surprisingly, the speaker turned it back on them and said, "You feed them."

And so, the team scoured the crowd with very little success in finding provisions except for one: our young boy.

The team brings his meager lunch, with the disappointing report, "Only five loaves of bread and two small fish." The enormity of the crowd at hand magnifies this disappointment. How could they feed such a large crowd with such little provision?

Their disappointment is because they had a scarcity mindset, and if we were there, we likely would have been thinking the same thing. They only had five loaves and two small fish. And that is not enough in the face of feeding such a massive crowd.

But their faith was in the provision and not in the Provider.

They failed to recognize that the small thing in their hands was more than enough to feed the crowds when placed in the creating, multiplying hands of the speaker, the Creator, the Provider of the provisions.

Of course, at this point, many of you know this story and how Jesus takes, breaks, gives thanks, and multiplies the meager lunch so that all the people, not just the 5,000 men recorded, but *all* the people are filled to their full...with leftovers!

What the disciples saw as scarcity, the crowd experienced as abundance!

Often when God calls you, God asks you to redeem the small thing you have in your hand. What is that small thing? What are you holding? The thing you don't think is worth anything, your meager lunch of five loaves and two small fish? When you look up from your hand and see the monumental need around you, the thing in your hand seems minuscule, it looks like nothing, and it is not enough.

And the great fear is that if you let go of this little thing, you will lose even that and be left with nothing. This is the scarcity mindset. There is barely enough for me, let alone for anyone else.

The great fear of the scarcity mindset is that if someone else gains because I let go of my one small thing, then all I have is loss.

Have you ever watched kids play the board game Monopoly? The game starts reasonably. Maybe there's a minor dispute over who gets the dog and who gets the thimble, and then it even becomes a little fun - some small purchases here and there - maybe a railroad or two. But you don't want to be around when the first big property gets purchased, because that is when at least one kid will immediately quit the game. They feel instant devastation and loss. They genuinely believe the game is over because of what they see someone else achieve.

How many of us have felt like this with our Kingdom Dream? We believe the lie that someone else's gain is our loss - that there are only a few colorful squares on the board of our life, and if we don't push our thimble to those squares first and have enough money to buy them before someone else does, we will lose our dream.

We are fed a lie that if you don't hustle and grind and strive, you will miss out on that promotion, that investor, customer, and dollar. Our kingdom dream turns into something that we can lose if you don't figure out how to beat everyone else. Suddenly the kingdom dream we were given that once was a gift has become an enormous burden that we have to fight for and protect and stay up late nights worrying about. The thing that was given to us to be our joy becomes our burden. But we forget that we are not bound to the scarcity mindset of this world or Monopoly. We walk in a different truth:

God Has Plenty of Resources.

We have found that there are two traps people fall into when it comes to money: the Poverty Trap and the Prosperity Trap. Sadly, both traps are where good dreams go to die!

The danger of the Poverty Trap is that people assume that it's somehow holy to not have money. As if there were some financial benchmark for how poor you are that equates to how holy you are.

There is a danger on the other side with the Prosperity Trap that equates God's blessing and your holiness to have much money you have! As if there is some sort of formula that if you pray enough, are obedient enough, and ask sincerely enough, you will be rich.

Real prosperity isn't about how much you possess but how much you can bless. God wants to give you provision for your vision.

❊ ❊ ❊

Taylor joined our KDI 4-Month Start-Up Incubator as a micro-church planter seeking a sustainable funding model that could perpetuate the life of his church community.

Throughout the process, Taylor wrestled with the tension of wanting to make an Impact in his community while simultaneously needing to make Income to sustain the Impact. Taylor landed on a non-profit strategy called Launch Local that would help hyper-local, community-minded entrepreneurs get their projects started.

At Pitch Day, Taylor announced Launch Local's first project: a mobile coffee cart that would be used to serve excellent coffee at community events such as baseball tournaments, concerts on the square and around their downtown area. Taylor and his team uses the mobile coffee cart to be highly relational with customers while simultaneously bringing in necessary income for the ministries of the church. The vision Taylor casted at Pitch Day was enough for an angel investor to donate $10,000 to Taylor's burgeoning movement! This was enough to make a purchase of the coffee cart and get Launch Local launched into the community.

It is hard for us to imagine that every single resource is at God's disposal, and we simply need to pray and wait for God to move resources into our corner to accomplish the mission that God has for us. It's not just about money; although money is a big deal for start-ups, God has all the resources to accomplish His mission for the world in the palm of His hand and is simply waiting for you to be ready to receive it.

When dreamers dream, we dream big! And sometimes we see the end before anyone else can see it. One of our participants could see that to get to the end of his project, it would require at least $300,000 to bring it to reality. This seemed like too much for this dreamer to overcome and so the dream, while not dead, fizzled for a while. At least until he was able to find a way to create a minimum viable product that would only cost $10,000 to launch. This was an attainable goal that givers were willing to donate towards to create a proof of concept that would be viable in future iterations.

Jesus talks in the Sermon on the Mount about not worrying about what you will eat or wear, God will provide for you. He says that God has provided for the birds and the flowers. How much more so does God care for you and provide for you?

Do you live in faith knowing that God will provide for you to accomplish the mission God has given you? Do you have an abundance mindset that says God has enough resources to make this happen? Or do you have a scarcity mindset that lives in fear, worry, and anxiety that there will never be enough to make your kingdom dream come true?

We must fight against our natural instinct, which binds us up in fear that we don't have the right funds, right relationships, and right skills at just the right time and place. But God is calling us to have faith. Faith over hustle.

God has given you a Kingdom Dream to birth something into the world; don't think that God won't resource it!

When we (Dave) launched our start-up we had very little outside funding. We scraped and scrounged everything we had to try and pull off the impossible. It got to the point where we had to make some decisions to purchase equipment that would empty the bank account. I can't tell you how scared I was to make that purchase, so I sought some wise counsel from a friend who was a few years down the road in his start-up. This friend asked me a few questions. He first asked, "Do you need this piece of equipment to run your business?" I replied, "Yes, we can't do it without it, but it will empty the bank account." He said he understood the risk, but then he asked a follow-up question that changed the course of our business, "Whose money is it in that account? Is it yours? Is it an investor's? Or is it God's money?"

Long story short, we purchased that piece of equipment, and not only was the money replaced in the bank account, but it also doubled within a few weeks! That's how God's abundance can work!

In the Bible, Nehemiah had a dream to fix the wall surrounding Jerusalem. This was an overwhelming task that he did not have the resources to accomplish, but he thinks through and asks these questions:

- Who does have the resources?
- Who might capture the vision?
- Who might be able to help me?

Nehemiah was able to gather all the right resources to rebuild the wall! Or maybe better stated, God gathered all the right resources to help Nehemiah realize the Kingdom Dream that God put in his heart.

Over and over in scripture, we find Jesus teaching this principle that it's not necessarily about our hustle or what we have but what God has and what God can do. Jesus fed 5,000 people from a young boy's five loaves and two fishes. Jesus told the parable of the talents, where people invested what they had and were given responsibility over greater things. God sent Moses with just a staff to confront the most powerful man in the world and ask Pharoah to let the

Hebrews go. As a young boy, David only had five smooth stones to defeat a giant.

God takes the smallest thing that we have and multiplies it for God's Kingdom purposes!

Hudson Taylor, one of the most prolific trans-cultural missionaries, once said, "God's work done in God's way will never lack God's supplies." God's resources are greater than we can imagine; the psalmist describes the vastness of God's wealth as owning cattle on a thousand hills. All the treasures of the world are at God's disposal. As Taylor might suggest, doing God's work is merely asking God to supply you with the supplies to do what God has called you to do!

But maybe God is asking: Where do you have your faith, in the Provision or the Provider?

A pithy quote that summarizes Isaiah 58:11 says, "Where God guides, God provides." The sentiment behind this is that we can trust that God will give us all the provisions necessary to accomplish God's will and work in every endeavor to which He leads us. We can take judicious risks for kingdom advancement. We can invest the resources we do have into the community.

We can do this because our God is a God of abundance, and God has plenty of resources.

The key is that you might have to trust in someone other than yourself. You must let go of the "pick yourself up by your own bootstraps" mentality so that God can bless you in the most surprising ways and places.

We aren't suggesting that you don't work hard or put in the effort. We are suggesting that you begin to create your business with God. Knowing that your work each day is your faithful offering to make the world a better place and knowing that God is in control. We are suggesting that you can't do it alone. Honestly, your loaves and fishes are not enough. You need someone else to come alongside you and give you the help, resources, and supplies you need for your Kingdom Dream to be a reality.

You have to let go.

Let go of your tiny resource so it can be taken, broken, blessed, and multiplied. Even if you don't have everything you need right now, you are one relationship away from funding everything. Our team is always reminding each other that one moment of God's favor is greater than a thousand hours of human hustle.

God is a God of abundance, and He has called you to this kingdom dream at this time and this place. God did not bring you to this point to leave you with nothing! God will give you the right resources at the right time to make sure the kingdom dream He gave you will come to life.

## Apply Foundational Truth #2: Relationship Mapping

To apply the foundational truth that 'God has plenty of resourcesFaith over Hustle', look at what you already have through God's eyes.

The practical tool to integrate this foundational truth into your life is Relationship Mapping. It involves mapping out all of your connections and relationships on a sheet of paper. This exercise is great to help us see how God has surrounded us with the resources and relationships we need to step into his calling.

## Step 1

On a sheet of paper draw a circle in the center and list your name within it. Then map out all of your relationships by adding in people you are connected with. Also, add in organizations such as your work or your church and the people connected to them.

## Step 2

Look at the names you have written, who are you connected with? What resources do they have? How can they help you?

# Step 3

Now look at where you lack. What relationships do you need to cultivate so that you are empowered to grow and develop?

Use the Relationship Mapping tool to regularly to shift your mindset from one that says "I lack" to one that says "I have" and to open your eyes to what God is doing in your life.

# PROCESS

*These truths will help you while you are on your journey to keep a steady pace and not burn out.*

# FOUNDATIONAL TRUTH #3

*Progress Over Perfection: You Don't Climb a Mountain in a Day*

> "There are no constraints on the human mind, no walls around the human spirit, no barriers to our progress except those we ourselves erect."
>
> RONALD REAGAN

> *Count it all joy, my brothers, when you meet trials of various kinds, for you know that the testing of your faith produces steadfastness. And let steadfastness have its full effect, that you may be perfect and complete, lacking in nothing.*
>
> JAMES 1:2-4

The disputed 2007 Kenyan presidential election erupted in violence. Estimates of up to 1,000 to 1,500 people were killed, and more than 350,000 people were displaced, primarily in the Rift Valley, where most of the violence was centered.

One of those people caught up in this turmoil and violence and displaced from her home was the 2022 winner of the New York Marathon, Sharon Lodeki. Sharon saw firsthand the effects of violence as a young thirteen-year-old girl. When Sharon finally returned home, she turned her attention to the one thing most young people from the Rift Valley turned to, running.

As a young girl, Lodeki would run three or four kilometers to school every morning and run home every afternoon. She developed a love for running and a thirst for education. Eventually, she saw running as a ticket out of the Rift Valley, as she had seen many competitive distance runners earn their way to spots with professional clubs worldwide.

Sharon Lodeki's goal was to receive an education and escape the poverty and violence of her upbringing.

During her seventh and eighth grade years, Lodeki discovered she had a gift for running that exceeded her peers. She was finishing at or near the top in most races and began starting at district and national races. At this time, Lodeki moved to a new school, all girls, about forty kilometers from home. Here is where she began to train with world-class runners who were winning races all over the globe.

In her efforts to keep up with faster and more mature runners, Lodeki started to dream that a career as a professional runner was possible. However, after high school, she found herself in a lull for about eighteen months with no international prospects for school. While she waited for college to begin in Kenya, she helped her mother's business. She worked on the family farm and cared for her younger siblings.

While she knew of others who had made it overseas for education and training, she could not imagine how to get there until one day when her uncle invited her to a running camp where a recruiter from the University of Kansas happened to be. By the end of the following year, she finished an improbable freshman season with a tenth-place finish at the NCCAA Cross Country Championships for the University of Kansas.

In 2018, Sharon Lodeki capped a phenomenal college career by winning the 10,000-meter NCAA Division I Outdoor Track and Field Championships. Her dreams of running and getting an education were finally realized.

Following this rise to stardom, Lodeki set her eyes on professional sports. She joined a professional running club based in Flagstaff, Arizona, where she now lives and trains. Her first entry to a marathon was in 2022, where she pulled off an improbable victory, winning by seven seconds.

Sharon Lodeki spoke of her frightful time as a young girl on the run from warring authorities, she said, "You leave everything. When you start running, you can't bring anything." For a whole month, her family lived in silence and fear. She and her family were in survival mode. They took each day as a gift and lived to survive the next day. Thoughts of winning marathons and getting an education in America were the furthest thing in her mind.

Lodeki had to learn to pace herself and take one step at a time to reach her goals.

As an entrepreneur, you have a voracious appetite for fast-paced, urgent attempts to conquer new territory and accomplish big goals. Most entrepreneurial leaders can only be satisfied once they have checked off the necessary items of achievement each day.

There are at least two problems with this typical approach to entrepreneurial life: 1) what you accomplish becomes your identity, and 2) this pace is difficult, if not impossible, to keep over time.

Your identity is not tied up in what you do, can do, have done, or haven't done! Your identity is solely valued based on your relationship with God through Jesus Christ. God wants to redeem you and adopt you. It doesn't matter how many mountains you climb and businesses you start, God loves you for you!

We have found this principle to be true: pace = empathy.

When you are running at such a pace coming up with new ideas, new goals, and new plans, not only are you unable to empathetically interact with the users of your ministry and your team, you are likely on a fast track to burnout in your own life! Sometimes the pace in which you run is actually more significant than the actual destination.

We have also learned that when we are hustling for

survival our survival instincts kick in. Every experienced entrepreneur knows what I'm talking about! The desire to win, succeed, hit that goal or make payroll becomes the only instinct you have. You completely and fully operate in survival mode. We can do that for a season but not forever. When we spend extended periods of time in survival mode we lose our *why*. We forget about the very reason we started. When we over focus on surviving we lose our ability to dream. Many of you have been there halfway up the mountain pushing through to survive one more day. When we find ourselves in this space we need progress not perfection. You just need to make progress.

Progress Over Perfection.

Oftentimes dreams die because they simply fail to launch. You keep working and working to fine-tune and perfect each little detail but then never actually ship your product or program to the market. You can keep building and building but eventually you have to put it out there! What's your next step? What's your minimum viable product that you can launch to make progress toward our goal?

When I, (Ben) launched Kingdom Dreams Initiative, it was an incredibly vulnerable moment. I had launched other things before, but this was the first time it was all on me, it was my name behind it - and I had no one else to hide behind! I had it all on the line.

My goal was to launch with the look of maturity and perfection in mind, so I did everything necessary to make myself and KDI look competent and perfect, especially for a young company. But as I mentioned in the opening chapter of this book, our first public event ended in near failure. I wanted to be at the top of the mountain, but in reality I was barely getting started on the journey. We didn't need to be perfect but we desperately needed to achieve some progress.

I learned I needed to make progress over perfection.

Climbers working to summit Mt. Everest do not scale those icy cliffs in a single day. In fact, reaching the summit often takes weeks as climbers ascend to base camps at increasingly higher altitudes to allow their bodies to adjust over time to the new realities of climbing at altitude.

Likewise, we aren't meant to climb the enormous summit of entrepreneurship in a single day. Most of our projects take a long time to fulfill or complete and can not be perfected in a day! Not to mention our pace needs to be such that we can handle living life at the altitude of the mountain we are climbing.

In his letter to the Philippians, the Apostle Paul writes about the slow climb of goals. In chapter three, verses 10 and 11, he states his goal:

*I want to know Christ—yes, to know the power of his resurrection and participation in his sufferings, becoming like him in his death, and so, somehow, attaining to the resurrection from the dead.*

Paul wanted to experience the power of resurrection at the high end and know what suffering and death were like for Jesus. In all ways, Paul wanted to become like Christ! That was his goal. But he knew he hadn't attained it yet. In verses 12-14, he says:

*Not that I have already obtained all this, or have already arrived at my goal, but I press on to take hold of that for which*

*Christ Jesus took hold of me. Brothers and sisters, I do not consider myself yet to have taken hold of it. But one thing I do: Forgetting what is behind and straining toward what is ahead, I press on toward the goal to win the prize for which God has called me heavenward in Christ Jesus.*

Paul recognized that he hadn't arrived yet. He was working his way up the mountain. He was making progress while not yet being perfect. He says he presses on, or in Greek, "to run swiftly toward," to take hold of that for which Christ Jesus took hold of him.

He wanted to grasp the grace for which Jesus took hold of him.

Then Paul wraps it up by saying he has a single-minded focus on the future, pressing on to win the prize of the upward call of Jesus. He doesn't look back or get distracted; he moves forward, one step at a time, one day at a time.

※ ※ ※

When our friend Stew joined our Kingdom Dreams Initiative 4-Month Start-up Incubator, he had a dream to mentor people who are involved in student ministry. He noticed that many were starting out in ministry, just like he started, young and without the moorings and maturity of stability at home. So Stew began working on Nucleus Coaching, a mentoring and support program for men and women involved in student ministry. Stew always had that end goal in mind, but it first started as a one-pager. Then, he took that one-pager and made a website landing page.

Plain and simple, Stew just started making progress. He

would take the next MVA – minimum viable action – to make progress toward the goal to help women and men in student ministry. Early on, Stew understood that he just needed to build the next step for his participants, not the last step. Eventually, over time, step by step, he was able to build the whole program based on what he was learning in real-time with his participants so he could be most effective in addressing their unique needs.

There is another angle to this idea: Sometimes, we get a God-sized vision that seems wholly unreasonable and unattainable. Sometimes a God-sized vision is entirely overwhelming to look at. You look at everything stacked against you and wonder if you have it in you to go after it – is there enough energy to do this monumental task?

As the old saying goes, "Rome wasn't built in a day." And neither were most businesses, non-profits, and ministries.We forget it doesn't happen in one, two, or sometimes even a hundred days. We look at others and see their success but suffocate our dreams before taking the first step. We must be patient and confident that God will give us the pace we need when taking the first step.

Jesus invites us to come to him and rest. Matthew chapter 11 reports that Jesus, who was tired and worn out, says, "Come to me and learn the unforced rhythms of grace for my yoke is easy and my burden is light." Jesus wants to take away the stress of the pace that leads to burnout; Jesus wants to remove the burden and give you something easy and light.

We often look across the fence, street, or town and ask, "How did others accomplish those amazing things?" And a good chunk of the answer is: "They had the right pace."

You will sometimes feel discouraged when something is bigger than you, but because you are the steward of the dream, you must find ways to sustain it. Remember that you are looking for one more step of obedience each day. We are looking for progress, not perfection.

Without a doubt, you need to have a destination for the road you are building. You need to know where you are going but don't need to get there all in one day. Pacing matters.

Sometimes it helps to think about the destination. What does the end look like? What is the view from the mountaintop? Write that down. What could happen here? What would the feeling be like when it's done? And other times, it helps to look at the next base camp. What next goal will help me get closer to the mountaintop? Write that down. What is the minimal viable action that will get you there?

And then just start making progress. One step at a time.

## Apply Foundational Truth #3:

To apply the foundational truth that 'You Don't Climb the Mountain in a Day = Progress over Perfection', combine planning with dreaming.

## DREAM + PLAN

| 5 YEARS | |
| 4 QUARTERS | |
| 3 MONTHS | |
| 2 WEEKS | |
| 1 DAY | |

The practical tool to integrate this foundational truth into your life is Ryder Carroll's 54321. It is an exercise you can do to connect your Kingdom dream to your daily actions. By dreaming big you gain motivation and a sense of which direction to head in. By planning smaller steps you gain clarity on what to do next which fuels your progress.

## Step 1

Dream and plan by filling in a 54321 by answering the following questions.

- **5 years** - what is your dream?
- **4 quarters** - what needs to happen in the next year to move towards your 5 year dream?

- **3 months** - what needs to happen in the next 3 months to move towards your 1 year goal?
- **2 weeks** - what needs to happen in the next two weeks to move towards your 3 month goal?
- **1 day** - what needs to happen today to move towards your 2 week goal?

## Step 2

Regularly come back to track and update your 54321. It can be used daily or sporadically on days when you are struggling to make progress.

# FOUNDATIONAL TRUTH #4

*Action Over Inaction: Have a Bias Towards Redemptive Action*

> "An idea without action is like a bow without an arrow."
>
> MARTIN LUTHER KING, JR.

> "Do you want to know who you are? Don't ask. Act! Action will delineate and define you."
>
> WITOLD GOMBROWICZ

Revered Union Colonel of the Civil War, Joshua Chamberlain started with humble beginnings. Raised on a farm in northern New England, the first of five children, Joshua was destined to become a minister, at least, if his mother had her way. He taught Sunday School, led the choir, taught himself Greek all while in high school. His parents taught Joshua to value education and eventually he studied Latin, German and mastered French and Syriac.

In 1855 Joshua married the daughter of a local pastor and they grew a family together. At this time, he went into education, first teaching logic and natural theology and later rhetoric, oratory, and eventually becoming a professor of modern languages.

Despite the years of study, theorizing and learning, Joshua was action-oriented. When the American Civil War began, he encouraged his students to follow their hearts in regards to their involvement. However, as the war continued on, he determined to follow his own heart and requested a two-year leave of absence, upon which he immediately enlisted unbeknownst to his family and administration.

As an educated man, he was selected as an officer and began training as a Lieutenant Colonel with the 20th Maine. The 20th Maine saw early action in the war in the Battle of Fredericksburg in December of 1862 but it wasn't until July of 1863 that our professor turned warrior would become a household name. At the Battle of Gettysburg, Colonel Chamberlain displayed uncanny leadership, bold decision-making, and a bias toward action that proved to be crucial in aiding the United States to victory in the gruesome battle which turned the tide of the war in favor of the North.

At a crucial point in the battle, having sustained heavy losses in his regiment, the 20th Maine had repulsed attack after Confederate attack. Ammunition was running low, men were lying dead across the battlefield and yet, Chamberlain knew the strategic importance of holding his portion of the field called "Little Round Top" which protected the entire left flank of the Union Army. As yet another Confederate attack mounted, Chamberlain recognized their desperate situation and ordered his men to fix bayonets, preparing them to charge the oncoming assailants in hand to hand combat. And charge they did!

This surprise action, albeit desperate, caught the attacking army off guard, resulting in a resounding Union victory with 101 Confederate soldiers captured and Col. Chamberlain himself taking a prisoner captive.

In those desperate moments, something needed to be done. The 20th Maine could not sustain another assault. They could not stay where they were. They could not freeze or pause. They couldn't do what they had always done and expect a different result.

Instead, Colonel Joshua Chamberlain rose to the occasion and displayed a courageous bias toward action that resulted in Union victory on that day in 1863 and some might say, the entire war. Over the next two years, Chamberlain rose through the ranks to eventually become General Chamberlain who accepted the Confederate surrender at Appomattox in 1865.

How did a farmboy in Maine go from being a teacher who knew 6 different languages to becoming an Army general who accepted the surrender of an entire nation? Not to mention, after the war, serving 4 terms as the Governor of Maine!

We think, in part, because Joshua Chamberlain was a man of deliberate action. He didn't just study, he acted. He didn't just learn how to deal in theories, he put theory into practice.

Oftentimes we study and learn but we don't act. We like information, we like to learn, we like content, but when it comes to running a new start-up company, ministry, or church, eventually we have to act!

Dreams die because we fail to act! We fail to actually do something about our dream. The tendency is for some to stay in strategy mode and never move to execute the strategy. It seems safer to work on a strategy that *should* work rather than activate the strategy to see if it *would* work.

There are far more ideas and dreams locked away inside the heads of people who failed to act than there are dreams that have been actually launched. And perhaps the only reason they failed to launch is because the person simply did not know what to do next.

What if Chamberlain had stayed on Little Round Top, hunkered down with his troops? They would have risked total annihilation by simply staying the course. They had to act and they had to act right now! It's entirely possible that Chamberlain didn't know exactly what to do next, but he instinctively organized his troops for one final great push.

Our encouragement to you is this: When you don't know what to do next, build into your instinct to serve people. Just serve people. That's a pretty good instinct to develop. Build into your life redemptive action and it becomes second nature to you so that the next time you don't know what to do, you will simply serve people.

Taking that next step, that action is risky. Clearly for the 20th Maine at Gettysburg and indeed the entire Union Army, there was risk to the maneuver! But, the risk to stay the same, the risk of doing nothing, was greater than the risk to act and make a change.

Certainly there is some kind of risk when doing anything new or trying anything new, but eventually the risks to stay the same outweigh the risks to make a change. What's the risk if we stay the same? What's the risk if we make a change to serve people?

❋ ❋ ❋

Mary worked in the wellness and coaching space for a number of years prior to joining the Kingdom Dreams Initiative 4-Month Start-up Incubator. She had started Etched In Your Heart to provide spiritual counseling and coaching to people who need assistance in their spiritual lives. Mary worked on a variety of ways to make her organization work, whether it ran as a ministry of a local church, or opened her own place or partnered with another organization. She had lots of options on the table!

However, as she began to explore each option, most of the

time a door would close. But that didn't stop Mary from taking the next step to explore the next option, and the next and the next. She could have gotten so discouraged that she could have given up. But Etched In Your Heart was so important to her that it was etched in Mary's heart to take action and keep pursuing the redemptive good that she knew was for her to do. Ultimately, she took the risk to do contract spiritual coaching on an individualized basis because the best thing she knew how to do was to serve people.

Too often, we get stuck; we become paralyzed by something that keeps us from moving forward. Sometimes this is strategy, sometimes this is opportunity, sometimes it's a lack of skill or knowledge. What is the thing that is keeping you stuck in idea mode? What is the thing that is keeping you from moving forward?

We won't always have all the right information necessary to be confident in the change we are about to make. And so we study, we learn, we gain content, we find information... but what do we do with all that information? What do we do with everything we have learned? At some point, we need to act!

It has long been said that one can not steer a stationary ship; it must be moving and have momentum for the ship to be pointed in the right direction. Of course, with modern ships now, some can steer while creating their own momentum. Either way, movement and momentum are needed to steer the ship in the right direction. Even if the ship is pointed in the wrong direction, it must start moving in order to make course corrections.

For us, the point is to prioritize Action over Inaction.

What is it that keeps you from taking action? What keeps you from moving? What keeps you from serving people? It is helpful to name the things that keep us from moving forward. While there may be others, we've identified four primary excuses for dreamers to not move forward with their dreams.

## Fear And Finances - Ignorance And Isolation

**Fear**
There is a lot of fear when stepping out into the unknown world of entrepreneurship. You are blazing a new trail; you might be going where no one has gone before. You might have an unproven concept. You might not know if your idea will even work in the marketplace. And so, many people stop moving forward because they fear the unknown.

Even with the best market research and all the due diligence you can muster before launch, there is fear of the unknown for what lies ahead.

What lies ahead might be the greatest fear of all: Failure. What if we fail? What if no one buys our product, uses our services, or joins our cause? What if we invest tons of resources, time, and money, and we lose it all? What if I sink my family into debt? What if I waste the trust people put into me? What if I look like a failure?

These fears (and others) keep us from stepping forward, taking risks for the kingdom, and living the dreams God has for us.

**Finances**
There might be the fear of financial ruin. Maybe you have a scarcity mindset. For this we will refer you back to Truth #2 - Faith over Hustle, God Has Plenty of Resources. Without a doubt, finances are a genuine concern. You should be concerned about finances! But there is a kingdom-minded way of thinking about finances where God's economic system operates on a different scale than the world's system.

You need to be aware of your start-up's financial needs, the initial start-up costs, the operating expenses. You should be aware of what people are willing to pay for your product or program - we like to say that if you can't give it away for free you won't be able to sell it! You need to know whether or not you need to be paid or if you have a staff that needs to be paid – is this a passion project for you or an economic engine?

All of these concerns have kept others from even starting their start-up!

**Ignorance**
Not knowing enough has prevented many people from launching their idea. They just don't know how to do it, they don't know what the next natural step is or should be. So many dreamers have a great idea and that's all they have because they don't know what to do with it to make their dream a reality.

In this case, ignorance is not bliss!

This is where our incubators have helped scores of people to have breakthroughs with their next step. They are able to turn their ignorance into information to assist in taking the measured and logical next steps to overcome the fear and the financial constraints in starting a new thing. This is consistently the feedback we hear the most from our start up incubator participants: "KDI helped me get unstuck by giving me a roadmap and guiding me to what's next."

One of the problems with a lack of information is that dreamers can also have a quest to try and know everything. They fall prey to Paralysis by Analysis. They analyze everything and act on nothing. At some point, with all the information you have gathered, you have to move!

**Isolation**
Isolation occurs for the dreamer at every level. In the pre-start-up phase where you just have an idea and it's hard to articulate, no one seems to understand what you are dreaming about, let alone believe in you to pull it off. That's a lonely feeling!

And then after you launch, you are a full-on entrepreneur. Every piece of your business rises and falls on you. You are the architect and the builder. You are the marketer and the shopkeeper. You are the bookkeeper and the janitor. You do it all! That's also a lonely feeling!

Isolation creeps in when we haven't allowed people access to our lives and to our start-ups. Entrepreneurs need a community of supporters and believers in them to help them overcome the threats of loneliness and isolation.

So how do we overcome the quadruple threat of Fear and Finances, Ignorance and Isolation?

First we must change our mindset. We have to have a renewed mind that isn't conformed to the pattern of the world which thinks in terms of fear and scarcity. Romans 12:2 challenges us, *2 Do not conform to the pattern of this world, but be transformed by the renewing of your mind. Then you will be able to test and approve what God's will is—his good, pleasing and perfect will.*

We have to change our mindset from thinking, "I can't do this" to "I can learn how to do this." Failure is part of the entrepreneurial journey, but that failure brings valuable lessons that help you pivot to make changes in your product or program that will only enhance future versions of your start-up. We have to remember that as believers we have a redemptive purpose in life and that God wants to move God's resources into the places where redemption is happening.

Once your mindset is changed from "I can't" to "I can" you will begin to acquire knowledge and start to build a skill set unique to your start-up. Utilize online resources, books, courses, master classes, join an incubator. All of these are ways to overcome the ignorance barrier keeping you from taking your next step.

Join an existing network of entrepreneurs in your local community. Or create your own. Your local chamber of commerce might be a good place to start, but if one doesn't exist, there are many online communities where you can thwart the isolation barrier. By regularly connecting with people who are (or have been) working on a start-up you will stay motivated, focused and combat those feelings of loneliness. Another option is to go a step further and sign up for our 4-month Start Up Incubator Program at KDI!

Have a bias toward redemptive action. You have to find a way to keep moving forward, to keep pursuing your kingdom dream despite the challenges and barriers that thwart your progress. Don't be the Chamberlain stuck up on the hill, be the Chamberlain that takes action to win the day.

## Apply Foundational Truth #4: Growth Mindset

To apply the foundational truth 'Have a Bias Towards Redemptive Action = Action over Inaction', shift your mindset when you are stuck to get yourself moving again. The practical tool to integrate this foundational truth is applying a Growth Mindset.

As we try new things we can get stuck when we realize how much of a gap there is between where we are and where we want to be.

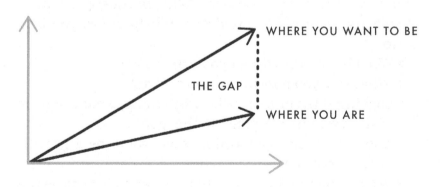

The entrepreneurial journey is filled with doing things you have never done before. When things might not work and we do not have all the answers we can slip into a fixed mindset.

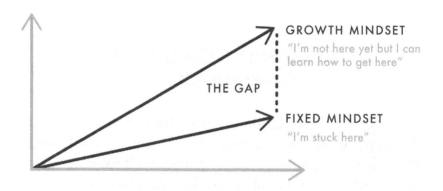

A fixed mindset believes that your abilities are fixed and cannot be improved ("I can't do this"). In contrast, a growth mindset centers on believing in your ability to figure things out ("I can learn how to do this").

When you get stuck, answer the following questions to see if shifting to a Growth mindset can help propel you into action.
- What is the desired spot you want to be?
- Where are you now in relation to that?
- Looking at the difference between those, what would be a fixed mindset response to that gap?
- Looking at that gap again, what would be a growth mindset response?
- What is one small action step you can take to close the gap and step into a growth mindset?

# POSTURE

*These truths will give you staying power in your work and help you build lasting relationships.*

# FOUNDATIONAL TRUTH #5

*Character Over Charisma: Your Dream Will Only Be as Redemptive as You Are*

> "Every action you take is a vote for the type of person you wish to become. No single instance will transform your beliefs, but as the votes build up, so does the evidence of your new identity."
>
> JAMES CLEAR

> Therefore, if anyone is in Christ, he is a new creation. The old has passed away; behold, the new has come.
>
> 2 CORINTHIANS 5:17

Mike Anderson was convicted of armed robbery in 2000, but that isn't the beginning or the end of his story.. The night of his crime, he and a friend were bored, tired, hungry, and angry. They followed a local Burger King night manager to the bank night deposit drop, where they robbed him of $2,000 at gunpoint. As a result, Anderson was convicted and sentenced to thirteen years of prison and released on bond. He was instructed that the State of Missouri would notify him and pick him up at some point.

Except, they never came to get him.

Anderson contacted his lawyer to see when they would come, and, interestingly enough, the state never picked him up to serve his sentence.

That's when Anderson decided to change his life for the good. He became a master carpenter, started a business, married, and had children. He started volunteering in his church, coached youth sports, and became an integral part of his community.

For thirteen years, Mike Anderson lived as a free man, building a community and becoming a productive member of society. He never moved, used the same address for his home and business, and paid taxes under the same name and address as a good citizen. By all accounts, Mike Anderson was a changed man from his youth when he first committed that robbery.

Until it was time for him to be released from his original sentence. In 2013 when the State of Missouri prepared the documents for Anderson's release, it was noticed that he was not in prison at all!

A warrant went out for his arrest, and eight Federal Marshals were sent to apprehend Anderson at his home, where he had been for all the preceding years. Anderson spent the next ten months in prison as his lawyers fought for his release.

At the end of this ordeal, the judge ordered his release saying, "You've been a good father. You've been a good husband. You've been a good tax paying citizen of the state of Missouri. That leads me to believe that you are a good man and a changed man. As such your sentence will be fully served and satisfied today.... Go home to your family, Mr. Anderson, and continue to be a good father, a good husband, a good taxpayer.... Good luck to you."

Mike Anderson was once again a free man.

Anderson quickly gives God the glory for his situation, recognizing God's providential hand throughout his life. But this story would have turned out much different had he not built new patterns in his life that would redeem his life and not return to a life of crime.

In his case, the judge rightly said of Anderson, "You are a good and a changed man." Over thirteen years, Mike Anderson did what the penal system is meant to do: rehabilitate and redeem lives. Mike changed the course of his life, and it was redeemed for the good!

All along this journey, we have been talking about bringing

systemic change into people's lives so that we can help solve a problem that people have. We want to see some change in their lives! But they can only change if we have changed too.

Too many dreams die because the dream becomes about you and not about other people. There is an entrepreneurial spirit out there that is only about the entrepreneur. They are out for their own success, not to bring success to the user of their product or program. This type of entrepreneur tends to over-promise and under-deliver thereby leaving a wake of pain and distrust in their path and then the dream just dies.

So the question becomes, how do we build this dream with the help of God and not on our own? How do we make it about the transformation of our users and not simply the glorification of self?

Corporate transformation always begins with individual renewal. If you want to change anything, it always starts from within. It must begin from within, if you want to change things in your neighborhood, it must start from within yourself and move out to your home and family and beyond to your neighbors. You can only change dynamics, situations, and circumstances for others as much as you have been changed yourself.

Many entrepreneurial leaders and pastors start new businesses, ministries, and churches, partly because the culture they were coming out of had some toxicity within. They have been part of a system that was destructive to themselves and to others. However, instead of redeeming that culture, they instead make the same mistakes and hurt people all over again just like they have been hurt.

We all know of organizations led by hurt people who hurt people. We all know of the charismatic leader who woos people into following them but their character is too weak to manage the responsibility of redemptive leadership.

This is why we emphasize character over charisma. You should spend more time developing your character than developing the attractional nature of your charisma.

When I (Ben) was a young man right out of bible college, I started as a youth pastor in Anderson Indiana. I loved my job, loved the kids, loved innovating new ideas and working with students. I was being mentored at the time by an experienced youth pastor who wasn't always generous with his praise. He in some ways saw me as competition and always had a critique for everything I did.

I preached one weekend in front of the entire congregation. It was probably a holiday or a weekend where the pastor was out of town. I had breakfast with the older youth pastor who said to me, "That was one of the finest sermons I have ever heard particularly from someone as young as you are." Then he said this and I've never forgotten it. He said, "be careful that you are never better in the pulpit than you are in your living room." He was saying to me that sometimes your gifts can take you to places where your character can't sustain you. Make sure whatever you do, you focus on who you really are not what you look like to others.

The requirement of creating a high-character culture is to slow down and build the margins, build the time, build the space, and build the system within your own life so that the fruit of the spirit can take root. Hustle culture is a lie;

waking up at five AM and making your bed doesn't produce any more results. Redemptively speaking, being connected with the Father and trusting the Lord's insights into your kingdom dream produces lasting results and change.

Building a fruit of the Spirit culture must start from within. Your leadership creates the culture that you have. Anxious leaders create an anxious culture. Angry leaders create a hostile culture. Indecisive leaders create a paralyzed culture. Unthankful leaders create a resentful culture. And on and on the list could go.

But on the other hand, redemptive leaders create redemptive cultures. Leaders go first and set the tone for the whole organization.

\* \* \*

Brittany took part in our Start-up Business Accelerator wanting to bring sanity back into the world of dance training. She had been fully immersed in the toxicity of dance culture for young girls and boys and desired to bring redemptive character into that world. So Brittany launched Illuminate Dance Studio which is dedicated to training the next generation and creating a non-toxic community that enables students to learn with freedom and illuminate any sphere they walk into.

And while Brittany herself oozes charisma, her character is of the highest regard and she is bringing a redemptive movement within the world of dance.

It is important to remember that you aren't just trying to redeem a problem for the people you serve; it's not just for the users of your ministry or business. You are redeeming the culture of your team as well.

You can create a redemptive culture for everyone around you - your team and those who intersect with your team's work. As such, that redemption starts with the work Jesus has done within you.

Ephesians 1:7-10 talks about the work that Jesus has done to redeem you and forgive you within the riches of Jesus' grace:

*In him we have redemption through his blood, the forgiveness of our trespasses, according to the riches of his grace, which he lavished upon us, in all wisdom and insight making known to us the mystery of his will, according to his purpose, which he set forth in Christ as a plan for the fullness of time, to unite all things in him, things in heaven and things on earth.*

Grace has been lavished on you to help you know the mystery of God's will and unite us all. What a powerful testimony to God's work through Jesus Christ!

But are you ready for the redemptive work of Jesus Christ to transform you so that we can begin redemptive work in others' lives? You can't lead people to a place you haven't already been.

The great Dallas Willard said, "The greatest issue facing the world today, with all its heartbreaking needs, is whether those who, by profession or culture, are identified as 'Christians' will become disciples – students, apprentices, practitioners – of Jesus Christ, steadily learning from him how to live the life of the Kingdom of the Heavens into every corner of human existence."

We do not have the luxury of skipping the margin of spending time with Jesus. People say they might be too busy; they don't have time for prayer, Bible reading, and journaling. Without a doubt, entrepreneurs are busy. Early in your start-up, everything is riding on you; you have a ton on your plate! But I would suggest that you are too busy NOT to pray. You have too much going on to NOT carve out dedicated time to be with the Father as Jesus did.

James Clear offers this advice, "You do not rise to the level of your goals. You fall to the level of your systems."

We must have practices and rhythms that help us be rooted with the Father, systems in our daily lives that give us the security of placing ourselves in a position for God to redeem. Identify areas where you want to grow with the Father and then cultivate that soil. Interestingly, we often try to grow ourselves, but try as we might, we can't grow anything; God provides the growth. The only thing we can do is cultivate the soil and prune the plant.

Be honest with yourself to develop habits for a good relationship with the Father before proceeding. If you imagine your start-up three years from now, what does it look like? How many employees or volunteers do you have? What do their lives look like? How many users of your start-up do you have, and what do their lives look like? But what about you? What does your life look like and your family? Are they still with you?

Your dream can only be as redemptive as you are. And now is the time where you make it so. Establish the patterns and systems now so that you are prepared and healthy when you arrive at your destination and your family and team are healthy. You can redeem the problems and situations people are in because Jesus has redeemed yours.

There is a concept of obscure fruitfulness. It's the stuff no one else sees but you and God. Do the work of cultivating soil and pruning your life regardless of who is watching. Be the one silently doing the unnoticed work. Develop a rule of life to sit and walk with Jesus. And develop disciplines of generosity and growth.

## Apply Foundational Truth #5: Spiritual Rhythms

To apply the foundational truth that 'Your Dream is Only as Redemptive as You are = Character over Charisma', incorporate spiritual rhythms into your schedule.

The practical tool to integrate this foundational truth is scheduling in time with God to your schedule. Spending time in Scripture, praying, and journaling are spiritual disciplines that will serve you in your entrepreneurial journey.

For your work to be as redemptive as you are, you must design your life with spiritual rhythms that will continue to refine and redeem you as you live out your Kingdom

Dream. If you design your dream but neglect to design your life around it, you will begin to neglect your own soul in service of the work.

## Step 1

What are your current spiritual rhythms? Be honest; it's okay if they don't look like what you want. How do they help you live a redemptive life?

## Step 2

What spiritual rhythms do you need to add in? What things in your life do you need to stop doing to make space for these rhythms?

# FOUNDATIONAL TRUTH #6

*People Over Profit: Invest in the Highest Return*

> "Assurance is the fruit that grows out of the root of faith."
>
> STEPHEN CHARNOCK

> And other seeds fell into good soil and produced grain, growing up and increasing and yielding thirtyfold and sixtyfold and a hundredfold.
>
> MARK 4:8

At work, Tim Johnson was the rock star employee on the fast track through management, eagerly climbing the proverbial corporate ladder. At home, he was a distant presence, occupied by business matters.

Late nights at the office, dinners with potential clients, and fifty, sixty, and seventy-hour work weeks all culminated in a potential to level-up in his to VP of Operations at one of the largest firms in his industry. It came at a cost that he didn't know he was expending. While he worked hard every day to provide for his family, unbeknownst to him, his family suffered in his absence.

Yes, each new ladder rung brought more financial benefit, but the big new house it bought was quiet, unhappy, and, what he did not know yet, unfulfilling.

It was February 2020 when Tim learned he was a leading candidate for the soon-opening VP position. This was a huge opportunity for him and his family. They could basically write their own financial ticket to whatever they wanted and needed. He could finally pay off all of the debt, he could finally purchase the dream car, and they could set their children up for life.

Yes, it would mean even more stress and time away from the family, but in the end, it would all be worth it for the financial gain, Tim reasoned to himself.

But then, mid-March of 2020 came through like a buzz-saw ruining all the plans that everyone had. The Covid-19 pandemic was blowing around the world, shutting down everything from pre-schools to Fortune 500 companies. Tim's company was no exception.

Suddenly the world was divided between essential workers and non-essential workers. As a mid-level manager, Tim was designated non-essential. He was to work from home.

There was a difficult adjustment for the Johnson family as Tim and his wife now had to navigate working from home and teaching their children with at-home learning. Use of the wifi, meeting schedules, and coordinating oversight of the children became areas of concern and conflict.

Emotionally, Tim had to reset his own expectations from being the rock star at work to becoming a role player at home. As the initial shock of the sudden changes wore off and the routine developed, Tim realized that his children were not mere dependents from a financial and tax standpoint but human beings with personalities, hopes, and dreams – just like he had.

Tim started to look forward to his part of the day with the kids. Every day at three PM, he was in charge of snack time. He started researching different snacks he could make to surprise and delight his children. What surprised him was that their delight became his delight.

At work, the retiring VP of Operations decided to delay his retirement to help the company through the pandemic interruption. The idea of the promotion was off the table for Tim for the time being.

Tim began to relish working from home, spending time

with the family, balancing work and rest rhythms, and becoming an integral part of his family, no longer providing with an outside role. This continued for over a year until the summer of 2021, when Tim's company announced they would return to the office. The company's President met with Tim personally to inform him that the VP of Operations position was opening back up and that Tim was the only candidate they were considering.

The president informed him that while Tim was a rockstar at work before the pandemic, Tim became a superstar working from home. And so, they tapped Tim to move one more rung up that corporate ladder.

Tim and his family had a huge decision to make: to lean into the new normal with a healthy family, healthy boundaries, and healthy work-rest rhythms or resume the old normal with the grind of work demands daily pressing into his limited schedule?

Millions of people worldwide are facing this exact problem, in fact, globally 70% of employees are declining promotions because they have learned that there is more to life than work.

People have learned this principle: When you say Yes to something, you are saying No to something else.

Tim had said "Yes" to his employer for all those years, which by necessity said "No" to his family. And then, in an instant, Tim was thrust into a home life that was unfamiliar to him but which he grew to love. Ultimately, Tim would join the 70% and say "No" to his work so that he could say "Yes" to his family.

There is more to life than work, than attaining the next

promotion and getting the next raise. There is more to life than landing the next contract, making more money for your company, and having the corner office.

In the Kingdom, success looks different than it does in the world. Jesus says we are to bear much fruit. Fruit is the success of the kingdom.

The world wants us to invest everything in making money to show that the highest level of bearing fruit is great wealth. But Jesus' Kingdom Way suggests that we can invest everything, our money, knowledge, skills, time, and relationships to see spiritual fruit in our lives and the lives of others.

Tim learned throughout the pandemic that there was more to success than merely winning at work. Real fruit was produced and harvested at home that was of greater value than anything he had ever done at work.

The sixth foundational truth is to emphasize People over Profit - invest in the highest return.

We want you to invest your time, energy, and resources into the places, people, and projects that move your start-up forward and bear fruit for the Kingdom.

In John chapter 15, Jesus provides the disciples with an analogy of branches that produce fruit so long as the branches are connected to the vine. He says, "I am the true vine, and my Father is the gardener. He cuts off every branch in me that bears no fruit,while he prunes every branch that does bear fruit so that it will be even more fruitful" (John 15:1-2).

Fruitfulness is the goal, but only possible when connected

to the vine...connected to God through Jesus Christ himself!

Aside from connection to the Father, there are two interesting and helpful principles in this short passage:
1. What doesn't bear fruit gets cut.
2. What bears fruit gets pruned.

Why is there all this cutting and pruning? Again, we look to the scripture. That which does not bear fruit gets cut because it is wasting resources, it is a dying part of the plant that is not benefiting the plant, nor is it benefiting anything outside the plant. Without fruit, it is not nourishing anything. It is not reproducing itself. It is a waste of valuable resources.

But why would something be pruned if it is actually bearing fruit? Jesus gives us the answer: so that it will bear much fruit or be more fruitful. Sometimes we need to prune away fruitful things in our lives in one area to be even more fruitful in others.

Dreams often die because the dreamer has chosen to follow the wrong fruit. They have chosen to follow the fruit of income and profit, forgetting that their redemptive dream is meant to impact people from a kingdom perspective.

Certainly many people have run successful businesses and even sold those businesses for enormous profits. Also, we may all know of people who look successful by human standards have suffered from burnout and frustration because they have followed the wrong fruit. They look to profit over people. They did not prune nor cut to provide for the right kinds of fruit.

Two questions that may be helpful in filtering out whether

you are in need of some pruning and cutting:
1. Is this dream redemptive for anyone beyond myself and my bank account?
2. Is this dream solving a real problem for real people?

If you answer no to either of these questions, we would suggest that's time to get out the pruning shears so you can give your start-up some pruning and return to seeing people over profits.

Pruning means we need to say "No" to something (even if it bears some kind of fruit) so that we can say "Yes" to something else so that it bears even more fruit.

This can be hard to do in practice because we generally don't like to tell people "no," especially when we are in the start-up phase and need anyone and everyone on board to make things happen! But we need to set clear and strong boundaries with some people and projects that aren't producing fruit or producing little fruit, keeping us from fulfilling the dream God has planted in us.

The Kingdom is about your yes, responding affirmatively to God's call, but your yes also means some no's. You can't –or at least shouldn't – say yes to everything, so by saying yes to one thing, you are saying no to something else. You might as well say no to the things that aren't bearing fruit!

You will need to be honest about some things you might have to give up to walk in your kingdom dream. Jesus says this is counting the cost, knowing what you are giving up, and knowing what you can take on to follow him well.

One of the first steps is to look and see what your Minimum Viable Product or Action would be. You don't need the perfect product, but ask yourself, what can I do? What action can I take that will eventually bear fruit? We want the highest return on our labor to maximize our efforts. How and where can I make the most impact with the least effort?

※ ※ ※

Ross is an incredibly talented artist and creative writer. Ross was an early participant in our KDI 4-Month Start-Up Incubator and his dream was to launch an app that would combine art and culture along with devotionals, music, meditations into one location for people to experience it all. His highest aim was to help people grow in their faith in whatever capacity they could.

But in working to develop his app, Ross realized that he didn't need to make his app make money. Ross has an enormously generous heart that says, "I don't need to make money on this, I just want to help people!" Ross is blessed to have alternate sources of income and therefore could make his dream a passion-project that he was able to work on in his down time. Ross' work came from a heart to invest in the highest return – people and to allow God to bring the fruit of that investment in new and creative ways.

Ross positioned himself and his app to produce the highest kinds of fruit – kingdom fruit -- by emphasizing people over profits. The branch of the plant doesn't produce fruit through effort. The branch produces fruit as the natural by-product of being connected to the vine. So what is your next best and easiest step?

The 80/20 Rule posits that 80% of our results generally

come from 20% of our efforts. If this is true, then what can we do to maximize our effectiveness to make progress toward accomplishing the mission. We like to ask, what's the one domino you can knock down today that makes progress to knock down more dominoes tomorrow? What's the investment for today that makes fruit for tomorrow? Then follow the fruit.

Dave Rhodes has said, "Most people are trying to change their environment, but what they need to change is their investment." When you invest in fruit, the environment will change over time.

Remember Tim from the beginning of the chapter? Tim was forced to change his environment at the beginning of the pandemic. Still, he was given the choice to change the environment at the end. But by then, he had changed his investment. He was fully invested in his career and climbing the corporate ladder. Then his investment changed to the higher kinds of fruit. When his investment changed, his environment changed.

Kingdom Dreamers are often looking for something else, something different, something better. We feel like we are not making progress or the fruit that we have isn't valuable or not the kind of fruit that we actually want.

I (Dave) had a pickup truck one time that only had rear-wheel drive. One day in the winter, there was no weight in the back, and there happened to be just enough ice on the road that I couldn't get any traction. I remember pulling up to a stop sign, and when it was my turn to go, I pressed the accelerator and went nowhere. My engine was revved, and I looked at my speedometer, thirty, forty, fifty miles per hour, and I was stationary!

Do you ever feel like you are spinning your wheels? Like you are going nowhere fast? Do you feel like your pace is high, your engine is running, but there is nothing to show? Like a pick-up truck on ice, it may be that you are investing a lot of your time and energy into things that don't return good fruit.

To invest in the highest return, we must follow the fruit where God is already producing. That may mean saying "no" to something. Count the cost of what you need to prune today to bear fruit tomorrow. Once you do, you will find yourself on a solid surface, making the kind of progress to take you where you need to go.

## Apply Foundational Truth #6: Decision Matrix

To apply the foundational truth 'Invest in the Highest Return = People over Profit', assess potential actions based on Kingdom impact and effort.

## DECISION MATRIX

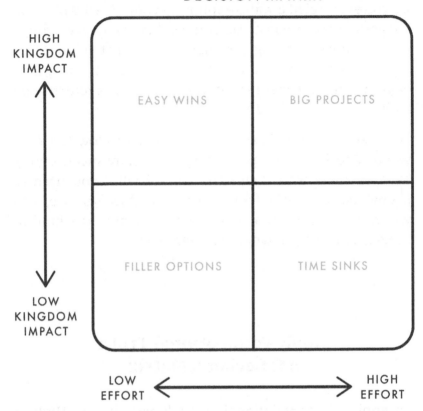

The practical tool to integrate this foundational truth into your life is the Decision Matrix. It can be used to assess a group of tasks, ideas, or projects to determine how to move forward. Simply plot a series of potential actions you are considering on the matrix to determine how best to steward your time and energy.

# FOUNDATIONAL TRUTH #7

*What Stands in the Way Becomes the Way Back: Resilience Over Resistance*

> "The impediment to action advances action. What stands in the way becomes the way."
>
> — MARCUS AURELIUS

> *Not only that, but we rejoice in our sufferings, knowing that suffering produces endurance, and endurance produces character, and character produces hope, and hope does not put us to shame because God's love has been poured into our hearts through the Holy Spirit who has been given to us.*
>
> — ROMANS 5:3-5

Born prematurely in 1916 on the banks of the Ohio River in Cincinnati to Italian immigrant parents was the unlikely start to the life of the record-breaking thoroughbred jockey Eddie Arcaro. During the Prohibition era, his father held odd jobs as a taxi driver and illegal liquor runner. As a child small in stature, under five feet tall, and just eighty pounds, Eddie was rejected from the baseball team, and he would never exceed five feet, two inches.

At thirteen years of age, Eddie dropped out of school to become a caddy at a local golf course, but try as he might, those bags were almost as big as his tiny frame! Working at the country club, he overheard someone saying his body type would be best suited to jockey racehorses. At his first opportunity, Eddie went to a nearby race track across the river in Kentucky and immediately got a job with a trainer. He dropped out of school and started making seventy-five cents per day training horses. He was too young to receive a permit to race, so he rode illegally until he finally came off at age sixteen.

He lost his first race. And the race after that. And the race after that. There was always something that would happen. His cap would fly off on this race, lose his whip on the next race, and nearly fall off the horse afterward. Word spread in the horse-racing world that he had terrible luck.

Eddie Arcaro had to start looking for a new trainer, but his reputation often preceded him; Eddie could not get out of his own way. He was described as clumsy and usually found to be in the wrong place at the wrong time. He was pushed and shoved, he was kicked and bruised, he was trampled on and bone-broken. But every time he healed up, Eddie got back on that horse to ride another day.

Some estimates say that Eddie lost his first one hundred races.

Until one day, the losing stopped. And the winning started. In January of 1932, at the Aqua Caliente track in Tijuana, Mexico, on a horse named Eagle Bird, Eddie finally got his first win - before he was legally allowed to ride! With a single-minded focus, Eddie began training with thoroughbreds in New Orleans and began excelling to the extent he was invited back to Kentucky to train.

In 1935, Arcaro rode in his first Kentucky Derby, and in 1938, he won the derby gaining him national notoriety. In 1941, Eddie Arcaro won the coveted Triple Crown by winning horse racing's three largest races: the Kentucky Derby, the Preakness, and the Belmont Stakes.

In 1945, Arcaro won the Kentucky Derby again, and in 1948, a Triple Crown was repeated. His retirement came in 1961 at forty-six after a stunning 4,779 wins, 3,807 second-place finishes, and 554 victories in stakes races.

Eddie Arcaro is the only jockey to win multiple Triple Crowns. He is tied with the most wins at the Kentucky Derby (five) and holds the most wins at the Preakness and the Belmont at six each. Such is the story of the diminutive son of Italian immigrants who could not find a way to win early in his life and career. The thing that stood in his way – an inability to win – became his way forward. New York Times journalist Joseph Durso said, "He rode with rare technical gifts, but mostly with an uncanny sense of mission that he seemed to share with his horse and a killer's instinct for winning."

He had an uncanny sense of mission.

He saw the obstacles as opportunities, and whenever an obstacle was created, he found a way to climb it and hurdle it to accomplish his mission of being the most decorated jockey ever. Eddie Arcaro illustrates the integral quality of resilience that must be present in every venture and every entrepreneur.

Resilience is adapting to and overcoming obstacles. It's viewing challenges as something that will help you learn, grow and improve rather than a limitation that will thwart your plans.

Ryan Holiday has done significant work with this concept in his book, *The Obstacle Is the Way: The Timeless Art of Turning Trials into Triumph*. This book explores the Marcus Aurelius quote at the head of this chapter, "The impediment to action advances action. What stands in the way becomes the way."
Holiday says that the secret to overcoming challenges is to reframe them in your mind, to turn the obstacle upside down so that what stands in the way in front of you becomes the way forward for you.

The diminutive Eddie Arcaro turned his slight stature into one of the winningest horse jockeys of all time.

Is your challenge a wall you can not overcome or a hurdle that propels you forward? The key question becomes how do we reframe adversity. It's not simply the moments and setbacks that happen to us that matter, it is the meaning we take from those moments. It's our ability to stand in the face of adversity and reframe those moments.

Sometimes we ask the wrong question, we ask ourselves, or God, why is this happening *to* me vs why is this happening *for* me. What we have learned is that the number one need for any entrepreneur is perseverance. We have a strange belief that the best ideas always win but reality teaches us that it's not always the best ideas but it is the leaders who, like Eddie, are willing to keep going, to reinvent themselves, to keep pushing and to try again.

The writer of the New Testament book of James is no stranger to challenges and struggles. Right at the top of his address, he mentions the reality of trials:

*Count it all joy, my brothers, when you meet trials of various kinds, for you know that the testing of your faith produces steadfastness. And let steadfastness have its full effect, that you may be perfect and complete, lacking in nothing.* James 1:2-4

He doesn't say "if." He says, "when." *When* you meet trials. The sad reality of life is that trials are an ever-present potential. Let's say it this way, if you aren't in the midst of some sort of challenge now, you will be soon! But the writer says to consider it a joy!

A joy?! Trials and challenges are supposed to be a joy? Clearly, the author has some warped views on life!

However, James indicates that trials or challenges give the believer steadfastness or "patience," as translated in other versions. The Greek word here for steadfastness is *hupomone*. It means patience, but it's not the kind of patience that helps you wait in the lobby of your mechanic while your tires get changed, instead, this is an enduring patience that enables you to finish a marathon.

*Hupomone* is bearing a heavy load without seeking to avoid or escape it.

Rarely do we ever have the experience that everything works out easily and as expected the first time. You probably recognize this to be true: most of the time, in life, in ministry and in business there are challenges and barriers that must be overcome. Success isn't a linear path. There's stops and starts, adjustments and "try again-s."

When my (Dave) team and I were working toward building our play cafe, we were promised that the labor would be provided by our property owner. We were renting square footage in a downtown block that needed major renovation along with all the future businesses in that block. However, due to cost overruns and labor shortages our landlord ceased working on our side of the project, with very little communication.

If we wanted to open in any certain timeline, we had to pivot, we had to come up with our own labor pool, we had to find building materials on the cheap, we had to develop partnerships with contractors and we had to learn to do things for ourselves.

We had to literally bear the load of the entire renovation project or risk never opening or waiting years to open.

There is more than one way to get to your destination, accomplish your task, and reach your goal. *Hupomone* can help you achieve that destination even when the challenges you face look like obstacles you can not overcome.

This is resilience: a steadfast patience to overcome obstacles as they appear on the horizon. This is vastly different from "resistance."

Resistance refuses to comply with or even accept the reality of the new challenge. The strength of resiliency is acknowledging the new realities and adapting to meet them head-on. Adapting to meet challenges head-on. Read that again. Adapting to meet challenges head-on. Resistance refuses to adapt. Resistance stubbornly stays the same, expecting the challenges to adapt to their stalwart refusal to bend.

There are times when resistance is necessary. Resisting mission-creep is always wise. Resisting moral failure is advised. Resisting oppressive relationships is necessary. But when it comes to facing challenges, it is almost always recommended to resiliently adapt to the changing environment.

Please dont hear what we are not saying. There is a lot of talk these days about grit, and we believe grit is a significant skill for dreamers to have, but resilience is not the same as grit. According to Dr. Taryn Marie, "grit is simply putting your head down and continuing to attack a problem by an act of sheer will and determination." Some problems can be solved that way, but not all of them. We prefer the language of *productive resilience*. It's knowing when to persist and keep pushing and when in the face of diminishing returns we stop pushing and fighting and we pivot.

Resilience is the ability to keep pushing wisely, not the ability to keep pushing blindly. Grit works in environments that don't change. If you want to lose weight, if you want to learn how to play guitar, if you want to run faster, grit works. There are times when environments are disrupted, shifting and changing and grit is not what we need, wisdom is what we need. Hustle culture says with every problem you simply wake up earlier, keep pushing, work harder and keep fighting. Productive resilience says sometimes you need to pivot, but what you don't do is to stop working the problem.

This is true for you personally and for your start-up or organization. Develop resilience to patiently bear the load as you adapt to new challenges. But how do you do that? How do you become resilient, aside from just grinding out life when you are faced with difficult circumstances?

We think, as with everything else, developing resilience requires intentionality. People don't drift into resilience, it takes effort and work. Consider the fives A's of resilience:

**Acknowledge Your Reality**
The temptation of resistance is to stick your head in the sand and refuse to accept that there is a new reality presenting itself. However, acknowledging your changing reality orients you to a position to face the challenge head on. Remember Eddie Arcaro from the beginning of this chapter? What if teenaged Eddie had kept caddying bags that were as big as he was? What if he stubbornly refused to acknowledge his diminutive reality? He would have likely worked his entire life trying to be someone he was not.

You have to acknowledge your reality and recognize the challenges that lay ahead of you.

**Accept Your Limitations**
You can't do it all and you can't be it all. You aren't equipped to do everything and be everything. You have limitations as to what you can do and even what you should do. Ask yourself, in the face of this new reality, what capacities and what competencies do I have to meet the challenge? Anything outside of your capacity and competency should be considered a limitation. For Eddie Arcaro, his height and size were a limitation, which once he accepted it, he made an enormous shift in his life. He couldn't carry golf bags, but horses could carry him.

From a Biblical perspective, the Apostle Paul characterizes limitations as weakness, that God's power is revealed in our weakness, our limitations. Accepting our limitations is part of becoming resilient, you can't carry all your bags – and other people's baggage – but you can allow God to bring people alongside you to help carry you and your vision through your challenges.

**Adapt Your Responses**
You have built in responses when challenges come your way. This is typically referred to as Fight or Flight response or more recently the additions of Freeze and Fawn have been wisely added. When you are faced with a new challenge, do you typically rise up and fight to face it head on? Or perhaps your tendency is to run from the challenge in the flight response? Or maybe you tend towards freezing where you feel paralyzed from moving and acting? Or maybe you fawn by having a tendency to people-please in

the face of challenge.

It is possible that any of these responses could be correct given the circumstances of your challenge. Resilience is knowing and adapting your response to the occasion. Sometimes you need to fight, sometimes you need to back down, sometimes you need to smooth things over and make people happy. Rarely does freezing help the situation!

Think about Eddie Arcaro adapting to his losing. He is the classic example of a fighter. He possibly lost over a hundred times. Yet after each loss, he got back on his horse and went back to work. That is resilience! But it may not always look like that – you have to adapt to your challenges, don't stay forever in your preferred response-mode.

**Adopt New Routines**
You have ingrained habits and thought patterns that have gotten you to where you are now. This may be a good thing, or it might be the very thing that has brought you a challenge! The good news is you can break old negative habits and develop new ones. You can learn new thought patterns.

Resilience may require a rewire of your brain! You need to be mindful of your thoughts as you face challenges and uncertainty. Some thoughts are just thoughts, you don't need to act on them. You can retrain your brain and develop new neural-pathways which will help you develop new habits.

Eddie Arcaro spent time after races pouring over his own mistakes to become a better jockey, but a shift occurred when he began scrutinizing the mistakes of other jockeys.

He changed his pattern, he adopted a new training routine and he became resilient to the losses.

## Advance Your Cause

You need to keep moving forward but with your new learnings. Facing a challenge may require you to make adjustments, but that doesn't mean you need to stop doing your thing! You have to keep moving forward! You have to keep making progress in your calling.

Resilience is advancing your cause in the face of adversity and allowing adversity to bring out the best in you. You can't avoid challenges, problems, issues, frustrations, they are a fact of human existence, however, you can rise to those challenges and face them with *hupomone* – patient endurance – so that your resilience is revealed in your character.

Some of the most difficult times in your life may be directly related to your entrepreneurial work. You can be so discouraged by the challenges that you face but through patient endurance you can adapt your work to fit the ever-changing needs and environment.

Resilience, patient endurance. These characteristics help us overcome the obstacles before us so that we reframe them into opportunities. What stands in the way becomes the way. This is resilience at its finest.

# EPILOGUE

You are about to embark on an epic journey! You have to start somewhere in order to prepare for that journey. We believe that these Seven Foundational Truths are the place to start before you start.

Just as a reminder from the opening chapters, they will help you:

1. Bear the load of the work you must do.
2. Anchor the structure of your organization.
3. Isolate outside influences from impacting you negatively.
4. Keep your structure square and plumb.

This is what good foundations do, but you have to *do* it. You have to create the practices in your life, you have to live out the principles in your life, you have to embed them into your start-up.

Jesus said that we must hear and do in order to have a solid foundation made of stone. We want you to apply it, we want you to do it. We want you to have a foundation made of stone!

We recommend that you take one Truth for every day of the week and make it your focus for the day. Give each Truth an entire day's worth of thoughtful consideration asking yourself, "How might I better live in this truth today?"

Think about if you started today and gave yourself seven weeks of seven days, each day focusing on one of the Foundational Truths, how much different would your life be? Two months from now we believe that your character will be changed! We believe your business will change! We believe your family will change! We believe that you can turn your life and your community upside down by living out the Foundational Truths intentionally and authentically.

Here they are, summarized below:

1. Fall in Love with the Problem Not Your Solution = Service over Strategy
2. God Has Plenty of Resources = Faith over Hustle
3. Invest in the Highest Return = People over Profit
4. You Don't Climb the Mountain in a Day = Progress over Perfection
5. Your Dream is Only as Redemptive as You are = Character over Charisma
6. Have a Bias Towards Redemptive Action = Action over Inaction
7. What Stands in the Way Becomes the Way Back = Resilience over Resistance

What will you do to take the next step toward your Kingdom Dream?

## JOIN A KDI START 4-MONTH START-UP INCUBATOR

### Our 4-Month Incubator Is The Best Way To Take The Next Steps For Your Dream!

DISCOVER your calling using tools to help you unlock your Person, Passion and the Problem you are meant to solve.

DESIGN a minimum viable product that will start to make your dream a reality.

DEVELOP a business plan that will give you long-term sustainability.

DEPLOY into the world through our Pitch Day and commissioning.

You will receive both one-to-one and group training along with access to our robust Mighty Network platform where you will find loads of resources and videos to help you make your dream a reality!

# START A KDI HUB IN YOUR CITY

KDI Hubs bring the KDI tools and coaches to a regional location near you! KDI Hubs help establish a kingdom-minded culture of entrepreneurship in a geographic region to support, guide, train, equip and inspire dreamers like you to make their dreams come true.

# HELP FUND AN UNDER-RESOURCED ENTREPRENEUR

Everyday dreams are dying because under-resourced leaders and entrepreneurs don't have access to the training, development and resources needed to launch their dream. The Awakening Dreams Foundation is a team of champions who serve these under-served leaders by training, developing and activating social entrepreneurs to launch their dreams. Since getting started in May of 2021, we have launched over 110 kingdom ventures, served over 700 entrepreneurs and launched incubators in multiple hub cities around the country. We believe we are

called to resource the next generation of dreamers so they can not only receive training and resourcing, but so they can launch their good work into the world. We have given away over $75,000 in funding and services to under-resourced dreamers. Please help seed a dream by supporting KDI with a one-time or monthly donation: www.kingdomdreamsinititative.com/foundation

## BECOME A CORPORATE SPONSOR

KDI has sponsorship opportunities in many cities across the country. Your company can become either a national or local sponsor helping support dreamers in your community or around the world! If you are interested in sponsorship opportunities: email ben@kingdomdreamsinitiative.com for more information.

Made in the USA
Middletown, DE
24 August 2024

59206465R00076